KNOW YOURSELF
THROUGH NUMEROLOGY

Meg Pringle Adamson is a numerologist and therapist who focuses on raising self-esteem. She is in private practice in London and gives seminars on numerology and self-esteem. She broadcasts regularly on radio. To relax she sprints and hill-climbs Aston Martins in motorsport, writes features for motoring magazines and loves travelling.

Know Yourself Through Numerology

Meg Pringle Adamson

HEADLINE

First published in 1994
by HEADLINE BOOK PUBLISHING

10 9 8 7 6 5 4 3 2

ISBN 0 7472 4543 6

Typeset by
Letterpart Limited, Reigate, Surrey

Printed and bound in Great Britain by
Cox & Wyman Ltd, Reading, Berks

HEADLINE BOOK PUBLISHING
A division of Hodder Headline PLC
338 Euston Road
London NW1 3BH

To Pythagoras
for sticking with it,
and to my mother for agreeing to deliver me to the
lessons of a master number 11 vibration

Contents

ACKNOWLEDGEMENTS

With very special thanks to my true friend Anne Cousins for letting me know the thing I did as a child was called numerology; to the thinkers' broadcaster Mike Allen for the radio show, and to the many hundreds of radio listeners who wrote to me in encouragement; to Sarah, Alan and Caroline for continuing to make Headline 'the gentleman's publisher'; and to my literary agent, Patrick Walsh, who's never there when you want him but always there when you need him; and of course, my loving thanks to Number for being constant even when we ignore its valuable lessons.

Part 1
Numerology starts here

What is Numerology

You have picked up this book out of choice, and it has the potential to enhance your life. If you can truthfully say that you are totally content to follow the pack, then put it back on the shelf. However, by reading on you *can* change your attitude towards life and yourself.

Numerology is about numbers, reincarnation, past lives, present lives and the lessons we have chosen to learn. It is the analysis of the numbers carried within a date of birth and the numerical value of each letter within a name. Numerology is a practical way of using these numbers we carry every day of our lives, whenever we need insight into a problem, need to reach for our highest potential, or seek to understand the personality of significant individuals in our lives. This book is based on Pythagorean numerology, with the addition of my own way of looking at numbers.

Numerology is not a random fortune-telling device, nor does it offend religions or creeds; it is neutral and at home within Catholicism, Judaism, Hinduism or agnosticism. It does not offer a god who may or may not return or trade your freedom for a ritual. Numerology, also known as metaphysical maths, is about potential and perspective and is a method of showing you how to exercise options *now* through deeper knowledge and comprehension of something you already have, and are recognised by: your date of birth and your name.

Numerology is about arithmetic; very simple adding and a little bit of subtracting. Numerology and maths differ enormously in that maths can tell you about your status, where you fit in – how much money you have, how tall you are, what you weigh. It cannot, however, tell you how you feel, how to cope or how to convert feelings into constructive energy instead of depression. Numerology shines a light on the very valid spiritual and emotional side of numbers which is usually ignored.

Throughout the centuries the knowledge held in the numbers contained within a name or a date has shown time and time again the lessons of the universe. Everything on the planet has a body, a soul and a vibration. The table you may be sitting at, the train you are on, the chair you sit in, all have a vibration, a meaning, a temperature, a texture. If your chair is wood it is made from a tree which knew how to grow. If the table is glass it is made from melted sand which was once rock in the seabed. That rock was, and still is, part of Mother Earth, but in a different form now. You too are part of Mother Earth, the universe, and you too have a numerological vibration, both physically and spiritually.

In numerology the soul is the pupil and the numbers indicative of the lessons we choose to learn. We each have a lifetime in which to progress and should we fail through avoidance or circumstance to learn the lessons, we become a non-progressed soul who will return until the message of universal order has been learned and understood. We can all think of someone who is an unhappy or unlucky person. It is more than likely that that person is avoiding the path he or she has chosen and is making heavy weather of the simple task of living their script and leading their life. Human beings, especially in the socially pressurised Western world, fall for the confusers of the planet who deliberately make us feel out of step, isolated, if we decide not to bond with or marry another, wear a certain style of clothing, drink a certain drink, live in a certain road. These confusers, the patron saints of peer pressure, place imaginary obstacles in front of us to make our clear life paths of experience and learning appear difficult. Don't fall for it. You came in with a hunger for the purpose of the lessons to be learned.

Living now and paying later always costs more than we thought at the time. Human beings can buy all the houses, sofas, designer clothes, fancy cars or take as many air trips as they like but staying home with your true self can be purgatory if you don't know who or why you are. The workaholic also comes into this category: working for the company, never for him or herself.

Numerology is swift, illuminating and available to everyone on the planet who can add up without having to take his socks off. The biggest aerobic you will have to practise if you are not confident about your arithmetic is pressing the + button on your calculator.

We will go into the meanings of the numbers a bit later in the book, but to give you a confidence-booster on how easy numerology is to learn, let me show you how to reach a life path number. The life path is the reason you are here, your purpose, and your number is contained within your date of birth. Our life path number, the most important number we carry, and one which cannot be changed, is found simply by adding the components of your date of birth together and reducing the result to a single digit. For example, 17/5/67 would first give you 36 (1 + 7 + 5 + 1 + 9 + 6 + 7 = 36). This double figure is then reduced further by adding the two figures together (3 + 6 = 9). So the life path number of date of birth 17/5/1967 is 9. The only numbers which are not usually reduced are the master numbers – 11, 22 and 33; and, in this book, 10 – but more about master numbers later. It's as simple as that to reach the relevant numbers, and it takes just a little bit longer to learn the meaning of each number. The book is a fun way of utilising one of the oldest analytical techniques in the world, and for all we know at present, the universe. It is a valuable tool which shows you how to gain a deeper understanding and a more comfortable perspective of yourself and others through the analysis of personality, potential and purpose contained within a date of birth and a name. The date of birth or name is not restricted to a person – it can be a company, the date on which it was formed, the potential of a certain date, a place, or anything.

So every one of us comes into this world with a manual in the form of numbers, which we need to know before we set out on our course. In the method we will be using you will need, until you are confident enough to do it in your head, a pen or pencil and a blank piece of paper. On that piece of paper we will make a simple empty noughts-and-crosses grid as shown below, which gives us nine squares into which to insert the chosen numbers.

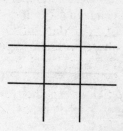

This keeps the numbers in a neat and easy-to-read chart. The numbers which are to be analysed and the nine boxes in which they sit are a condensed identity to which people can relate in times of crisis or when making a major decision. As we will see in detail later on, each example of any figure from 1 to 9 is always placed in the same box, as shown below:

3	6	9
2	5	8
1	4	7

The grid for the birthdate 12/4/1967, therefore, would be laid out:

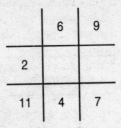

In numerology there is a simple format, a bit like a Chinese menu – a complete experience neatly abbreviated to a number. The next time you go into the Chinese takeaway you may think 'I had 7 last time I was here; it's delicious, but I think I'll have 22 this time.' Numerology allows you to choose your life path lessons *before* you come into the world. The next piece of information may surprise you, so hold on to your hat and consider it. Before we are born, at the in-between-lives stage, we choose our family, our spouses and our lessons to learn from as part of perfecting the soul. The family is described in the dictionary as 'a group of things related by common characteristics or properties'. Before the child's soul transmigrates into each life it knows what the lessons it chooses to learn are and the family it can learn from. It is believed that the child even chooses its name. The family – the university – collectively known as Brown has begun a new branch and the process of growing up, the meeting, the falling in love, cohabiting or marrying, conception and parenting continues as new members join their numbers to those of the others already there or on their way. Read this last section again and allow the knowing within you to be released. This knowing is not new – it has been there for all time, but pressure from power-seeking others has tried to dismiss it for centuries.

Throughout the centuries, people such as Plato, Socrates, Pythagoras, the sage and healer Empedocles, St Augustine, the ancient Hebrew Qaballah and Count Louis Hamon (alias the latter-day numerologist Chiero), have been recorded, some fleetingly, as mortals who understood the significance of numbers to our lives.

Two and a half thousand years ago Egyptian and Babylonian priests were using numerology as a descriptive and prescriptive for understanding human beings; centuries before them the Chaldeans were the tutors and messengers carrying numerology. Pythagoras is generally accredited as the father of numbers, yet in truth he is a son of numbers (the initials of which are SON). Who knows how different mankind would have turned out if numerology and its advantages had been understood as essential human knowledge from birth? A simple set of numbers to show you who you truly are. What joy – every human being recognising the pleasure and pain of their own script and learning about mankind in the process.

The spiritual side of numbers has been here all the time for us but somewhere along the line we have been restricted to viewing them in mere mathematical terms. We take influential exams and qualifications in Pythagorean mathematics, yet we are not, it appears, able to qualify in his equally important contribution numerologic, or numerology. By pushing the quantitative and omitting the qualitative, we have developed a 'never mind the quality, feel the width' society, curiously in the name of progress. Pythagoras, however, took his students into the universe with their minds.

Scholars and philosophers through the ages have used the Pythagorean method and the more ancient numerology of the Chaldeans, the mystics who inhabited Babylon, to gain insight into and illumination of the meaning of life, and the purpose, patterns and potential of mankind as part of the universe. We can learn much from universal law – the way things are – which is straightforward, orderly and perfect.

Pythagoras is associated with the idea Know Thyself (although it probably came from his teacher and mentor Thales; others say it came directly from Apollo, who also advised 'Nothing in Excess'). Yet for all we know it could have been a wise old Director of Urine Pots from Delphi one hundred years before them who should be credited. What is important about Know Thyself is that you are the only person you will ever truly know. Thales believed the universe was orderly, repetitive, and reliable and this has been proven: night follows day and winter follows autumn. As part of the universe we have the right to be the same.

How is Numerology Applied Today?
I have kept this book as close as possible to my estimation of and respect for the spirit of Pythagoras, who believed that everything is number and that to know number was to Know Thyself – yourself. Pythagoras was reputedly the son of the god Apollo (as were many others because of the God's predilection for the pleasures of mortal flesh). His birth was said to have been forecast by the Oracle of Delphi and his name, which his students are reputed to have used rarely because of its

sacredness, is in itself interesting. *Pytho* is the ancient name for Delphi, which was for many centuries the most famous place of worship and clairvoyant wisdom. The second part of his name, *Agoras*, is Greek for a popular gathering-place; a place to discuss what's going on. The Greek word *Python* means the spirit of divination (perhaps the serpent in the Garden of Eden was wiser than he was given credit for), and the Priestess Pythia was the channel, the orator of Apollo, the god of prophecy, who was reputed to be the bringer of answers from the gods to the questions of mortals on Mount Parnassus, Delphi. Those of you familiar with Greek history will be familiar with the Oracle of Delphi. It is interesting to note that Pythia, the seer, sat on and spoke the word from a tripod in Delphi and those who wished to consult her had to travel from their own far-off lands. Pythagoras's life path – his purpose – appears to have been that of the roving oracle for Apollo and other gods in order to spread their word further afield: how to keep on your life path with the help of the number.

Like the rest of us Pythagoras had to start somewhere, and in his mid-teens he furthered his life path by studying with the masters of knowledge in Phoenicia, Eastern Asia and Mesopotamia, broadening his knowledge through his studies and extensive travels (it is said that he spent over twenty years learning from the wise masters in these lands). With the Chaldeans and other teachers, he studied both mathematics and matters of the spirit, and through his curiosity and intuition made a connection between the two. He then returned to his birthplace, Samos, at around forty years of age to relay his precious self-knowledge through teaching in his own university. As his masters had done, he passed down this sacred and powerful knowledge by word of mouth. His students consisted of two factions, listeners and tutors. Students were first taught to listen, and only when they had succeeded in becoming great listeners could they be elected to teach others. Pythagoras was also the first man to refer to himself as a philosopher, the true meaning of a philosopher being someone who seeks wisdom and truth.

In modern terms, 'You've really got to want to do it,' coupled with 'I'll decide if you would use my knowledge for its true purpose, before I tell you,' may sum up the reason for the possibly sensible, but to the fearful, clandestine shroud which surrounded numerology until the early- to mid-twentieth century. Pythagoras lived a simple life, concentrating on matters of the mind. People sought his advice and his way, and because of their own ignorance and fear of his knowledge, those in power on Samos viewed him as élitist, a plotter against the state – in short, as extremely dangerous. They spread rumours about him and ridiculed him, and eventually the pressure of mob scorn forced him to leave Samos with his mother and some devout students for the Greek colony of Crotone in southern Italy. Again, perhaps the time had come for him to move on and to spread his wisdom in other lands, for surely he left something, a vibration and knowledge, in Samos which could never be lost or destroyed. In Crotone his calm wisdom was much welcomed during the backlash against its previous decadent leadership and he soon began his Pythagorean Brotherhood, where men and women enjoyed a rare equality in learning.

His teachings spread the potential contained within numerology and the intricate proof of deduction through mathematics into the ears and hearts of men. What better way of spreading truth than making the receiver of it responsible for getting it right? Pythagoras's 500BC method of learning to listen before practising or teaching, and being responsible for your own actions and words, reminds me of a twentieth-century story I heard about a jeweller. He suspected one of his staff, a person with a reputation for the big fib, of stealing. His problem was that the man was the black-sheep brother of the company's owner, and so clever was he that the jeweller couldn't quite prove anything. He had an idea for a way round this and immediately made the suspect head of diamonds, which involved counting the stones every night with a spot check whenever the manager chose. You may not be surprised to learn that nothing went missing again during the suspect's tenure. Like Pythagoras, the manager made the carrier of the knowledge responsible for being sensible with it and not distorting its true value, ownership and meaning.

As far as we know Pythagoras wrote nothing down. This may have been a deliberate act to ensure that, as his teaching passed down through the ages, each person who passed the knowledge on had to take on the responsibility for its truth. There has been no tampering with a piece of papyrus hundreds or thousands of years later to leave us scratching our heads and wondering, 'Did he mean this or did he mean that?', as has happened with some ancient texts. This method allows the serious student to seek out and develop numerology through thought analysis and development. He believed that everything has a resonance, everything is number. To this end we have a colossal beginning.

Who in the world really knows what Pythagoras, Socrates and Plato really had quiet hunches about? When those sages were developing and expanding numerology, knowledge was power and one wasn't really encouraged to go around shouting that one was cleverer than the Emperor: freedom of speech guaranteed freedom of the mortuary. We know from history that Socrates was charged with lack of respect for the state and put to death for impiety. Socrates' teacher Anaxagoras's rational theories made the religious leaders blow a fuse, but he was a bit luckier; he was merely banished from the land.

As a numerologist I can remind others of the importance of their lives through their numbers and can highlight a potential route for them to travel. My method and accuracy is important, but my personal opinion of their lives is not. The carrier of the numbers knows in his or her subconscious which path to travel but can be waylaid by powerfully destructive others and seek to be redirected to his or her destiny.

Like barcodes we are known to our governments as numbers, our cars have coded letters and numbers, our homes generally have numbers – even in a village we are 'third or fourth house on the left'. The personal numbers we carry are a special sequence of numbers, a compass reading for the road we have chosen to travel this time. In major dictionaries the first letter, consonant or vowel, in each section is related to the rest of the alphabet by being numbered to show readers the numerical location in the pattern of the English alphabet. For example: 'G – the seventh letter of the English alphabet. The fifth note of a C-major musical scale.' So Pythagoras was right: everything is number.

12

The reincarnation theory that we choose our parents and family in each lifetime holds good in numerology. It is like working within a university of learning, observing and learning how others handle life at close quarters. What purpose has a university with no fellow students or different subjects they are learning?

Numerology is used by some psychotherapists, personnel departments and GPs as an invaluable tool in understanding the behaviour, potential skills and weaknesses of patients and interviewees and to give an insight into significant people in our personal and professional lives. Parents of dysfunctional children can also make use of numerology to gain an understanding of which aspects of the child's character or skills to nurture. Often it is the case that a parent's learning curve and his or her offspring's coincide to teach both a lesson in tolerance and relating.

The daring it takes to stand up and say you believe in the potential of numerology is substantial simply because the pack mentality is so encouraged in our species that it is easier to be pushed around than to think around a problem. History is littered with the insults of unprogressed people who have hassled, jeered and persecuted those who tried to get a labour-saving, humanitarian, or factually advantageous idea across. One personal incident I recall involved an irate stressed-out accountant who asked me at a function why someone so talented, attractive and respected in the world of the mind could put her fine name to such tripe and trash (note the big complimentary build-up before the jab). I asked him which school of numerology he had studied and he surprised even himself when he replied, 'none'. I was able to smile and tell him the difference between his type of accountant and a numerologist. He reduces information to fit; a numerologist allows potential to expand into infinity.

Carl Jung spoke of racial memory, the collective consciousness which contains ancient knowledge; all that has gone before in the development of human beings. Where does our natural fight or flight response come from? That feeling when we are afraid, when the hair on the backs of our necks stands up, our pupils dilate so that we can see everything and our bodies break out in a cold sweat? We also are instinctive in feeding: a baby instinctively turns towards the breast when hungry, whether or not the person who is holding it is its mother; the toddler does not give up trying to use his legs to crawl and stand up, such is his need to get to something which has captured his eye across the room. Granted, he mimics the behaviour of adults, but the abused and ignored child is also an example of this will to experience: he remembers how to walk from somewhere. Everyone on the planet can access racial memory and *Know Yourself Through Numerology* offers an expansive odyssey into understanding, reawakening and activating intuitive use of something you *already* know and have. Instead of waiting for newspapers and television and radio bulletins to keep you informed of what has just happened, look back into the treasure chest of your mind and use the information and knowledge contained there to enlighten, progress and show you what *is* happening.

As I have said, this book is based on Pythagorean numerology, together with my own method of looking at numbers, which centres on the belief that the soul transmigrates into many different lives in order to perfect itself through learning and experiences. The evidence I offer for the possibility of reincarnation, from my experience as a psychotherapist using hypnosis in past life regression (PLR), comes from examining the between-life experience of the person regressing. Past life regression was a part of my psychotherapy studies which held little interest for me. I thought it a bit gimmicky and I am convinced that we can't consciously remember our previous lives because the present one is always the most important. Wouldn't it be horrendous if we were experiencing an extremely painful existence now while in the previous one we had been a wealthy, powerful prince or a burden-free, happy person? We would waste our time longing for the old life and not progress. Some people do that in their present lives; they hanker after someone who has chosen to leave them and who technically has no place on their life plan now: look at the spinster who gives up on the mating game because one experience of rejection was painful. We are responsible for our own happiness, not any other human being. The forty-year-old man who could have gone far if it hadn't been for his parents. He's an adult now, so what's stopping him?

Although I appreciated that many current personal problems or symptoms could be resolved and released respectively through careful analysis of emotions in past life regression, I was less excited about it than fellow students. Other students persistently asked me to 'do a PLR' on them but I avoided it like the plague, preferring the route of Jung, Freud and Milton Erickson. Early in private practice I did a couple and the word spread. In fact a pattern was emerging: PLR was refusing to let me go. In the light of later work in numerology I now know why. Everything has a reason, a purpose for being learned, endured or avoided. My lesson was that past lives, present lives and numerology are a family, a procedure in understanding evolution, not losing our thread. Pythagoras believed in the transmigration of the soul into many different lives. Each lifetime has the same soul but a different body; the soul is timeless, while the body lasts for only eighty to a hundred years if we are lucky.

In PLR it is essential when the subject enters a past life to accompany him or her through the dying process of that life in order to keep the journey true and clean in the racial memory. With many subjects I explored the feelings and impressions in the between-life state. The running theme was not one of awareness through seeing – rather the knowing and feeling were paramount. Almost without exception each person spoke of a warm wind and a spiralling upwards, with a purpose, or towards something or someone. They couldn't see it, they didn't have to, they told me; they knew, and that was enough for them, to know. Perhaps that was why Pythagoras wrote nothing down but awakened this knowledge within those who would and could listen.

In the between-lives state the calmness of the subject's voice communicating the information is noticeable and the realisation that the embryo soul is *choosing* to come through to this set of people and circumstances is exciting. There have been subjects who have reported with apprehension why they have had to come through to current pain, and once out of the hypnotic state were able to expand their understanding of their childhood lives in the present lifetime at a conscious level. Heavy words? Of course they are if it's the first time you've heard them. And like you, I am cynical of the people purporting to be Nefertiti, Cleopatra or Jesus Christ. In the regressions I have witnessed not once have I met a star of those bygone years. Going back to one of our previously mentioned occupations, where are the urine pot officials of Delphi? It was such a useful job because in ancient Greece the urine was left outside homes to be collected and used to keep the togas white. I would like to meet a quality controller of such a laundry in a regression.

The more you think about numerology, consider it and explore it, the lighter the burden of the information becomes. I do not ask you to believe it, I ask you simply to look at it for your own benefit and expansion of your thoughts about life. Numerology is not about setting out to change the world to suit us, but it can show you how to change your *response* to the world and to allow your purpose to contribute to mankind and enlighten you in the long term. The time taken up by what we shall eat tonight, tomorrow or on Saturday hijacks the time and energy which should be used for the work we are doing in the big picture – reality.

There is a marvellous slang retort, 'Get a life!' Well, we could do worse – in fact we do. We fall for stress, consumer competition or illness; we refuse to consider sticking to our own script, our own menu of numbers to be learned. Why is it that harder seems to be easier? I want what he's got and if I can't get it the way he got it I'll steal it. And it's not always just the junkie or the lush who gets it wrong.

Imagine, if you will, a beautiful woman going to a spectacular ball. She sits next to the Queen of England at the dinner, dances with the President of the United

States at 10 p.m., is invited by Clint Eastwood to star in his next movie at 11 p.m. and wins a Ferrari in the charity raffle at midnight. As she is leaving a guest accidentally spills a glass of red wine on her ballgown. The next day when her friend asks her whether she enjoyed herself her first comment is, 'It was a disaster, my gown got stained.' This lady has a perspective problem. By getting in touch with what she chose to learn in the beginning she could again see the doughnut instead of the hole. Through numerology we can connect with the format we have chosen to work to, and relate to problems as contrasts, an opportunity to have another go and get it right.

It is important to remember that there is never failure in life, only learning. We are constantly in a brand-new moment, and that's the exciting news.

By staying in constant touch with your present, and by acknowledging your potential you can choose, yes, choose, to leave the planet when your time comes with your potential at least enhanced, at best realised. That's a guarantee, if you can find the strength to mind your own business of minding your own numbers instead of trying to poach the life paths of others. In numerology we have the meaning of every number from 1 to 9 plus the meanings of the master numbers, which are 11, 22 and 33. I also use 10 as a master number.

These first facts are the gateway to never-ending potential and experiences. The most inspiring fact is that from basic beginnings of understanding we always have infinite possibilities. One small example of doing things the hard way would be the simple act of constantly tolerating people we dislike at our dinner table and forcing a long-term relationship out of a liaison which is

18

never going to go anywhere. Many marriages and business partnerships tread this unnecessary road of pain, mistrust and restriction. By looking at a chart we can see the differences between two people and the potential for failure as a couple. Life is a sequence of adventures, not a series of demands. Everything we need to know about ourselves is in and around us. The orderly, perfect universe to which we and Mother Earth belong is available and nurturing, and when adhered to enhances our progression as souls. The ancient study of the significance and analysis of numbers is a way of showing an individual how to realise and activate his or her potential through the analysis of the numbers with which he or she came into the world: the numerical vibration contained within the date of birth which is known as the life path number, and the numerical value of a name, which shows the persona, psyche and ability numbers.

We can change our names by deed poll, our faces by surgery, but we cannot change our dates of birth. The numbers on that day are etched in fact, and in most countries recorded on paper or computer for the rest of our lives. The vast majority of documents we have to fill in during our lifetime require us to reveal our names and our dates of birth for identification purposes.

Numerology acknowledges the deeper value of our lives, giving us a chance to understand ourselves for ourselves instead of seeking approval according to the scoring systems of others. We have produced a society which measures in discomfort for not conforming. Numerology allows you to find continued purpose in your life; to keep your own counsel and sanity on the planet. Symbolically we wear these birth numbers every day of our existence, and if we paid more attention as a species to the recognition and self-analysis of these precious codes we carry, we would gain a basic understanding of why we get into certain relationships or situations, which would be of great assistance to us.

It is important to understand that numerology should never be forced upon others or used to embarrass them. When broadcasting, I choose to discuss only the caller's potential strengths, rather than destroy his confidence by mentioning weaknesses. The feelings of the receiver should always be of paramount importance. A few words spoken in 'showspeak' can wound another's self-esteem, so it is important to tell the questioner that a more detailed reading could be given privately.

When you are showing someone how to expand into greater self-awareness and self-esteem through numbers they are also being challenged at some level by their roots, the role model for their existence as a human being. These usually incorporate some spiritual belief and teaching. There can be some inner conflict – the real self is questioning the information it has been fed by both sides; religious roots versus taking responsibility for the self. Yet no god, no matter what religion, would ever chastise those who seek more knowledge about life through themselves.

Remind yourself of the many times you have heard that human beings have x amount of space unused or uncharted in their brains. Numerology gives you another opportunity to traverse some of that space, to use the brain for the purpose for which it was designed, as a library for a universe of knowledge that is within each human. You have the ability and the right to access any information. What you don't have the right to do with it is interfere in someone else's life script. Mind your own script is the message.

Reclaim Your Right to be You
I cannot make you believe in numerology – nor would I wish to make anyone do anything. What I can show, though, is a simple, unflowery and effective method formulated from the fragments which have been handed down to gently release the special awareness within you. We all have access to the knowledge of numerology; some of us just shout a little louder from the rooftops about its worth.

Many numerology students bemoan the fact that Pythagoras left little in textual form and caused confusion or left gaps in the teaching of the art. I do not believe this is the case at all. By bequeathing a word-of-mouth skill he left room for the students to add their theories and expand the subject down through the centuries. It may also be that, like the wisdom of Tibet, numerology had to be fragmented to preserve it, and sections of Pythagoras's work went in separate directions when the university at Crotone was sacked by a mob led by uninformed zealots who hated the secret world of the Pythagorean Brotherhood, its calmness and its knowledge. As in the case of Tibet after the Chinese invasion of the 1950s, the world knows more about Tibetan Buddhism than it would if Tibet had remained a Shangri-la. The universe seems to force things to happen to ensure the spread of knowledge.

My message is learn the basic, and, just like your own life, nobody will do it better. Because it has so little ancient literature, numerology has a Garboesque quality. People might say it's a load of rubbish but still want to have their numbers 'done', so that innate wisdom is being prodded at the mention of numerology's potential. The foundation of numerology is so simple, clean and truthful, yet writers get away with bamboozling unsuspecting readers and publishers with hearsay. As for me, I'm sticking with the potential of numerology – awareness, guidelines, potential and truth. I don't recall Pythagoras the Video – not even on Betamax. I can pick up books on what *might* have been said or somebody's theory on what *might* make a good read, but there is only one way to relate to numerology and that is to do it.

Something does puzzle me, and that is, where did Pythagoras get it? To me numerology is not a unique gift, it is a universal gift for everyone, perhaps Cartesian in essence: 'I think, therefore I am.' Pythagoras either brought it here on a mission from somewhere in the universe (don't shoot me, I'm only looking at the options in Greek history and mythology) or was a psychic channel. In many encyclopaedias he is listed as 'a mystic who believed in the transmigration of souls,' a process which embodies the belief that we reincarnate to learn and perfect our higher souls. It is quite empowering to consider that we are in charge all the time and not the pawns in some other adult's game of restriction or destruction.

When in the sixth century Pythagoras settled in Crotone, he inaugurated his élite Pythagorean School of Philosophy which taught and sought the ultimate connection with the divine. Do not automatically confine yourself to the most obvious meaning of divine: to divine is also to find something intuitively, as in a divining rod searching for water, gold or oil. The best advice in the learning of numerology is to think left, right, above, below and behind as well as straight ahead, and you'll have got it just about right. The letters of the word 'divine' have a numerical value of 9 (we will see later on in the book how to find the numbers of names or words), which is the number of harmony, humanitarianism and bringing together.

The purpose of this book is to encourage you to learn from the spirit of the masters and develop your individuality. Don't believe numerology, that is restricting. Consider it and remember, we constantly live in a different moment of evolution. This book will give you the ground rules to eventually produce numerology the way *you* do it. A ridiculous number of humans seem hell-bent on perfecting a way of interpreting only one aspect of truth so that they can make it fit logic (commonly called physics). In doing so they restrict and abort their innate skills of expansive thought and ability. Rearrange the letters of physics, add an extra C and you get the word psychics – and if you really want to push it you will notice, when you have found out how to calculate the numerical value of letters, that the two letters you change, C and H, equal 11, the master number of the psychic and light.

Numerology appears on the surface to restrict human beings to nine categories, plus the master numbers. Yet in doing this the law of reverse effect comes into play, for through the seemingly narrowed opening into understanding, a flood of knowledge awaits the interested. My favourite example of the law of reverse effect is why is it we can walk across a three-foot-wide plank of wood when it is on the ground, but are frozen in terror when it is placed between two skyscrapers? If we can do it at one level why not at another? Remember this for the rest of your life.

Cast your mind back to Jung's racial memory, the part of our subconscious which remembers how to be a human being, and think about how a human generally behaves. Imagine the first inhabitants of earth and how uncomplicated they were. We may assume from archaeological evidence that they were few and far between, whether you Adam and Eve it or subscribe to the theory that we all got up one morning. Today when we communicate with a stranger we think more deeply about that person than we do about people in the street who are just passing by. Freud tells us that we first observe that the stranger is either male or female, secondly we establish whether we know him or her, and then thirdly whether we like him. We assess much faster than your eyes could read the last sentence.

By considering that there are really only a few types in human behaviour, but types with several stronger or lesser aspects or traits, then we can comprehend how simple the human species is in reality and how easy it is to get back to our script of numbered lessons to be learned.

Think of your grandmother. If you never knew your grandmother take a relative or guardian you know well. She may be seventy-five but it will not take you seventy-five years to describe the many different things about her. Many of the facts of her life will be repetition. Same house, same job, same partner, same thoughts, same habits. You will describe her by physical and behavioural traits, and quite quickly.

Exercise this with the next observation of behaviour and how it relates to numbers. Let's take for example the following couple. Jeff is a fifty-five-year-old steel worker from Sheffield. He was born on 16/7/1937, life path 7, he's analytical and knowledgeable with a potential capacity to impart much wisdom to others. He is a son, was a school pupil and later a trainee steel worker. He is now a qualified steel worker, a husband and the father of two girls whose upbringing he has little to do with because he thinks that's his wife's job (his mum said so). He watches television too much, goes to the pub every Friday and Saturday, doesn't like romance – it embarrasses him – but thinks Sheffield Wednesday are the top football team. He went to Dorset for his holidays every year until he was forty-six, when he ventured on a foreign holiday to Majorca. He now goes there every year, and to the same hotel, for his annual two-week holiday instead of to Dorset. His wife, Ann, was born on 24/3/1937, master number 11 life path. She's intuitive, inquisitive and energetic with a potential capability to delve deeper into the meaning of life. She wishes Jeff would break his routine and find something interesting to do. She gets angry with him because she thinks he restricts her. It never occurs to her that she allows him to restrict her. He says she nags, and avoids her by going to the potting shed to smoke his pipe, tend his racing pigeons or read a skin magazine.

Their potential as a couple is a 9 vibration, one of harmony and experiencing life in many ways, bringing information together for others if operating positively. If operating negatively, however, there is indecision, irritability and frustration. Both are scared to continue to change as individuals, even though both are desperate for the other to do something to make a change. Both feel it wouldn't be right in society's eyes to change outside the marriage, so they don't change at all. They just get sick through stress. Two life paths blocked by society's expectation or their own misinterpretation of what marriage is.

Who Can be a Numerologist?
The answer, in a nutshell, is anyone who can count. This numerologist began as a five-year-old who thought that people, houses, cars, buses and trucks looked like numbers. Many years later I learned that what I was doing was called numerology when a new friend, who does it in her own way, did my date of birth. A few months later she handed me an A4 sheet of paper on which was hand-written the meaning of the numbers. It came from her late father, who had used numerology in his practice as a psychotherapist. Here again is confirmation of the information being passed by word of mouth and of its simplicity. The information filled only half the piece of paper. I then bought some books and, without hesitation, I disagreed with some of the formats I read; eventually, I perfected my own method. So you see, Pythagoras had the right idea. He did it his way and left the students to develop theirs. As a child I had learned more about people by associating them with numbers and in hindsight followed the not-yet-tainted purity of a child by instinctively drawing from universal knowledge. Western stress and society drain our instincts in favour of financial gain and negative competitiveness. We become so embroiled in scraping a crust or a million together we forget our natural and effortless skills in living our lives, including all the historical blueprints we can call upon, numerology being one of them.

Perhaps Pythagoras did it the same way, trusting in accessing universal knowledge.

The purpose of this book is to encourage you to learn from the men and women who had to follow their insight in secret, and in doing so helped to illuminate your individuality. A Jungian analyst studies the way Jung did it, a Freudian analyst the way Freud did it. If they adhere to the rules without bending they become second-hand analysts. A good analyst learns from the big boys and adds his or her own 80 per cent. Remember, we live in a different moment of evolution. Pythagoras is reputed to have driven himself slightly bonkers trying to find the final lesson, the final frontier of the universe. I feel he failed to realise that infinity is within the individual and a brick wall to any another person. We can never perceive the full life of another but we can glimpse his path by the numbers he carries and understand our place in his world. Through numerology and the transference of this knowledge we can help others in need to get back on the right track.

Modern American psychologists Bandler and Grinder, the major developers and promoters of Neuro Linguistic Programming, or NLP, and the beloved Milton Erickson, who was practising techniques like NLP thirty years before it was called NLP, teach that life is simple. They highlight the fact that people waste so much time not distinguishing between being confused and not understanding. Confused means you already have a bunch of facts and are retrieving them wrongly. Not understanding means you have never learned how to do something. We spend a lifetime trying to make an unrealistic relationship, job or dream come true and forget that we have all the tools to access our potential in that area. If we gave as much attention to the detail in the numbers we carry, which highlight what we are supposed to be learning and acknowledge who is wasting our time and precious energy, the path would be so much smoother. Forget twenty years in analysis – people want answers about their purpose in life and they want them while they can still enjoy the benefits of them. Numerology is about the beauty and ability within us all. Only a psychopath or a charlatan would use it to depress or degrade another human being. Everyone knows what they are lousy at, but few know what they have the potential to be great at.

It is my intention to help create a brand-new numerologist within each reader and expand numerology into its rightful space. There is a common myth that numerology is a science and that the psychic side is abhorrent. I cannot seriously believe that a good numerologist does not use intuition. Every single moment of our day is dependent on intuition, the decision-making factor in all of us, the 'What do I know as a human being?' part – the internal tutor. This book is about numerology and cosmic awareness flowing freely between the subconscious and the conscious. Only the ego, the overworked and sometimes domineering gatekeeper to the conscious mind, can jam your frequency.

Students on my courses have used phrases such as: 'I never knew there was so much information about everyone in these "menus" ', 'Numerology has taught me my hunches are right', 'Numerology has changed my life' – numerology was always there, but they activiated its potential – 'Why haven't I heard about it before?' 'It's opened up a part of me I didn't know I had.'

Many people are born around 3.25 p.m. on Monday 10 May 1993, but few are called Elizabeth Jane Johnson, are they? Your date of birth and your name, maiden and married, all have a numerical vibration. Numerology covers all these factors. I have been fortunate enough to have met a few who have met others with the same date of birth, and in one case an English guy who worked with an Australian guy who was born at approximately the same moment as himself Down Under. Both worked in the same unusual branch of the medical profession, both had grown beards, both loved travel. Both were life path 1. Both had chosen to live at opposite ends of the meaning of 1.

The names, however, told the difference and the difference was that the Englishman read about travel and the Aussie travelled, one was scathing the other caring. The scathing critical one's name reduced to a 9 and the caring one's to 7.

The scathing one was curious about the other to the point of intrusiveness and the caring one tried to understand but in the end asked for a transfer from a job he loved. Numerology is an invaluable aid in understanding the moods of others, their actions or behaviour. When it is studied and interpreted properly, we can learn to work with or decide whether we desire to continue or invest in enhancing certain relationships with significant others in our lives, including our children. Number doesn't lie: a badly trained numerologist can, and a blocked person may not recognise his true path, but the numbers are constant.

To learn more about your life path, your strengths and

potential, follow the simple instructions in each section. Before you begin your journey into numerology allow your intuition to guide you by opening up to your own potential as a numerologist with a clear mind, an eager heart and the best intention.

Part 2
How does Numerology work?

Each number from 1 to 9 has a meaning; each letter in the alphabet has a numerical value from 1 to 9 and each value a meaning. 9 is the culmination because numerology works in a nine-year life cycle. In numerology it is widely supposed that 0 has no value. Most of the ancient scholars deny the value of 0, but I subscribe to the importance of 0 as evidence of an ancient skill brought through into this lifetime from a former lifetime, probably the previous life. Two 0s appear in an 8. The top 0 is the spiritual world; the lower is the earth.

MASTER NUMBERS
There are in addition three master numbers: 11, 22 and 33, which carry an extra lesson to learn or message to impart. They apply when a date of birth or name vibration reduces initially to a straight 11, or 29 (2 + 9 = 11) or 38 (3 + 8 = 11), or a straight 22 or 33.

Master numbers do not automatically make the carrier any better, richer or more enlightened than other numbers. The master number is a special path but it can be painful, burdensome and lonely. Its lesson can only be learned by diligence, and the incorporation of spiritual work or understanding. As a species we have a strange concept of what master means, and in numerology only truth counts. Master in its true sense means leadership, understanding of matters local and universal. It requires a lot of energy and courage to think huge and act huge. Numerology has a compensatory factor, and that is that when the going gets tough for the master number it can be reduced.

For example, if you are a master number 11 who feels that the numerological interpretations of 11 just do not 'click' with you, then you are finding the lesson of the 11 too exhausting or are denying your life path 11 potential. You may choose to reduce 11 to the $1 + 1 = 2$ vibration to live under. 2 is the number of service.

If you are a master number 22 then you may reduce to the 4, the number of order and detail (which, if operating negatively, holds the potential for chaos and duplicity).

A life path 33 is the most difficult number of all, and there are few people who truly carry this vibration. We can learn from the saint-like characters of those who can.

In this book the number 10 is also used as a master number whose meaning, like those of the other numbers, will be explained later. Like other master numbers 10 may be reduced, to 1, if it doesn't seem to fit.

Each individual number in the date of birth or name carries a message. It is not all about a condensed set of figures: each number stands to tell a tale on its own.

THE MEANING OF NUMBERS

Each number from 1 to 9, plus the master numbers 10, 11, 22 and 33, has a range of meanings and potentials for achievement. It is important to remember that there is no such thing as a bad number – every number has a positive and negative application and it is a matter of metaphorically flicking a switch to make beneficial change.

The following list of descriptions sums up the meaning of the numbers on three levels: over the top (an over-powering vibration), ideal and too low (a negative vibration), which helps to illustrate this vital point.

1
OTT: Bragging, defensive, loud-mouthed, selfish
Ideal: Entrepreneurial, independent, leader, active
Too Low: Lazy, blaming, negative, nervous, apathetic

2
OTT: Demoralising, sneaky, hypercritical, gossip
Ideal: Trustworthy, welcoming, gentle, loyal, warm
Too Low: Accident-prone, bland, sleeps too much

3
OTT: Liar, cheat, manipulator, smothering, unfo-cused
Ideal: Caring, lovable, outgoing, forward-thinking, humorous
Too Low: Bad-tempered, attracts lame ducks, put upon

4
OTT: Manipulating, indispensable, narrow-minded, rigid, intense
Ideal: Specific, clearly focused, neat, honest, reli-able
Too Low: Bamboozled, neurotic, everyone's out to get him

5

OTT: Theatrical, demanding, bombastic, libidinous

Ideal: Respects freedom, passionate, sensitive

Too Low: Restricted, prevaricating, nervy

6

OTT: Low self-esteemed, sceptical, debtor

Ideal: Family oriented, complete, generous, committee-lover

Too Low: Uncoordinated, bigoted, frigid

7

OTT: Prying, power-seeking, know-all, withdrawn

Ideal: Analytical, teacher, mystical, sturdy

Too Low: Hermit, gawky, social misfit

8

OTT: Narrowed, squabbler, coarse, snappy

Ideal: Honest, thinker, provider, home-maker

Too Low: Worrier, unseeing, no sense of purpose, low morals

9

OTT: Vain, uncommitted, self-seeking

Ideal: Sharing, caring, wise, harmonious

Too Low: People-pleaser, liar, distant, unavailable

Master Number 10

OTT: Wingeing, blaming, traitor

Ideal: Resolute, focused regardless, willing to take responsibility

Too Low: Lazy, frightened, worrier

Master Number 11

OTT: Socially impotent, unstable, unsure

Ideal: Dippy, nurturing, teacher of higher mind, universalist

Too Low: Liar, cheat, detests noise, lost, sad

Master Number 22

OTT: Despotic, inflicts cruelty, fanatical, collector

Ideal: Benefactor, business doyen, powerful, organised

Too Low: Foolish, turgid, lives too much in the head

Master Number 33

OTT: Interfering, destructive, martyr

Ideal: Healer, psychic, warm, witnessing

Too Low: Negative, physically stooped, never has time

Life Path Number

This is derived from your date of birth and is the foundation of what you are and the road you must travel to complete the journey of this lifetime. It is non-negotiable, it is unchangeable. It is called a life path for a very good reason: when you go on a journey there is a particular route you must take – you can try the side roads and short-cuts, but generally you will go in a particular direction. You cannot physically travel north from Edinburgh in Scotland to reach London in the south-east of England. OK, Smartypants at the back of the class, you could if you went via John-o'-Groats, the Arctic Circle, Antarctica, South America and across the Atlantic Ocean. Good point, though.

Why would you want to do it via such a difficult and arduous route? The life path is the motorway sign, the route-marker, and like Smartypants, many people choose an unnecessarily painful route to fulfilment.

Later you will learn how to read the date of birth in three sections: the day, the month and the year of birth.

Persona Number
This is the number which we prefer to show the world. The persona is the outer self which we generally feel is accepted by society. The woman who never ventures out without her eyes made up, or the bald man who always wears hats to hide his baldness, or the punk rocker who tries so hard to rebel, but who is in fact conforming to a uniform of leather, skin perforations and pink hair.

Psyche Number
This is the real you. The you that only you truly know, the secret self. It is derived from the vowels within your name. When we do not transmit clearly what is important to us, it can be very difficult for others to treat us in the way we would like to be treated simply because we are so unclear ourselves of what we are. Through understanding what drives us, we can reframe the message we transmit to others.

Ability Number
This shows how we can best express ourselves and our capabilities. This number, sometimes known as the name number, when fully understood, complements the life path number. It is derived from the numerical

value of a full name at birth, highlighting natural skills and abilities. Sometimes we are unsure of what we are good at, truly enjoy, or where we fit in in the employment stakes. By analysing this number we can encourage our latent talents.

THE LIFE PATH NUMBER

The life path is your purpose this time round on the planet. It is unchangeable, cast in stone. It is the collective marker-post, the light on the life path to take, a guide to the lessons of purpose. The life path number is calculated by adding all the digits of your date of birth individually then further reducing them to a single digit or master number in the way we have already discussed. For example, date of birth 11/9/1974 is $1 + 1 + 9 + 1 + 9 + 7 + 4 = 32$; $3 + 2 = 5$. The numerical value of the example is 5, the number of freedom, expression and respecting freedom.

For birthdate 23/7/1956, $2 + 3 + 7 + 1 + 9 + 5 + 6 = 33$. Remember that 33 is a master number and must not be reduced any further unless the carrier is finding it difficult to carry. Then the further reduction of $3 + 3$ would be 6.

The message from a master number which arrives via a 29 ($2 + 9 = 11$) or 38 ($3 + 8 = 11$) is a delayed reaching of the master number potential through circumstances within or beyond the carrier's control. An example which shows itself repeatedly is the intuitive side of an 11 coming to fruition via a 29 or 38 reduction at a later stage in life. The student is encouraged to analyse the meaning of the 2 and 9 in 29 and the 3 and 8 in 38. In doing so, the extra lessons to be learned en route to the master lesson will become apparent. The master numbers have a special significance, and the extra lesson they hold for us can be comfortable or uncomfortable, depending on whether it is acknowledged.

The student must be aware that even though the life path number is extremely important, the numbers in the whole date of birth are imperative to understand. Like a motor car, we might know it is an Alfa Romeo but what kind of Alfa Romeo – which model is it? – is more intriguing.

The meaning of the life path numbers and master numbers are as detailed below. As I mentioned earlier, many numerologists postulate that zero has no meaning in numerology. Not so. The zero is a complete cycle consciously brought forward to assist and enhance this lifetime. The zero may manifest itself in an awareness or interest in a certain period of history; perhaps an understanding or interest in weaving, morris dancing, jousting or the playing of a clavichord, lyre or zither.

1

You are motivated, persuasive, bold, ambitious and enjoy the position of being the boss whether in the home or in an employment situation. In childhood you may well have been entrepreneurial – as a paper boy or girl, for example, you would have delivered come rain, hail or shine. Working with a 1 can be fraught as they have a strong desire to be top dog, to be right. At their best they do make excellent leaders, but at worst they are tyrannical and selfish.

Advice: Promote
Avoid: The crooked deal

2

Good old reliable 2. A trifle touchy, you hurt more than others when subjected to loudmouths and bullies. Your sensitive nature must never be taken as bland, for those who take time to scrape away the sweet exterior will be pleased to find a stalwart, loyal and able companion or colleague. 2s are good listeners, affectionate, caring and prefer the quiet life to the bright lights or too much adventure. They are excellent at handicrafts, and particularly enjoy making things for the home. Because of their sensitive natures 2s tend to prevaricate and live very much on the fence. Sleep is an escape for the depressed 2.

Advice: Speak up
Avoid: Loudmouths

3

Unlike the 2, you love life in the fast lane. Karaoke is a godsend to the 3, who is up with the lark and home on the milkfloat. 3s must guard against burning the candle at both ends every night of the week. They can get into just as much of a rut going out every night as they can staying in. They must also learn that it is safe to be on their own and not constantly on the run. When they are not too busy having a good time they are masters of appearances and the sunbed will soothe their battered egos until the next plane ticket can be purchased. Because of their gift of the gab and ebullient nature, 3s attract all sorts of waifs and strays. They must be on their guard against time-wasters and malingerers who will gladly play on their kindness and regale them with lists of ailments and tales of woe for years on end. The 3 must learn the art of selective

company to reach his or her true potential.
Advice: Look before you leap
Avoid: Duplicitous individuals

4

You are the mental aerobics champion of numerology. 4s possess a calculating soul and are the royals of detail. Security is of prime importance to 4s, not only for themselves but for their families. They sell themselves and their skills by example and are often head-hunted in the world of commerce. The 4 is on the whole a tidy animal and lesser mortals are encouraged not to feel inferior when the fastidious 4 tidies up around them, even in their own homes! The 4 is often a workaholic and must watch his or her vitamin levels and sleep patterns while forging ahead in the ambition stakes. Generally everything they undertake they complete to the best of their ability.
Advice: Delegate
Avoid: Apathy

5

The flirtatious, popular 5 uses the clock on a twenty-four-hour basis. The only worry 5s appear to have on the surface is where the next piece of entertainment is coming from. At times they are self-centred, full of their own importance, and once this is pointed out they mellow for five minutes then proceed to do the same again. Yet they are generous to a fault and others find it difficult to stay cross with them for long. 5s have a tendency to gain weight, not surprisingly in the light of their lifestyle of fun, food and fantasy. They are constantly on the look-out for stimuli and a potential partner would do well to keep half a dozen reserve ideas up their sleeve for wet Sunday afternoons. Travel, writing and theatre are the world of the 5, with special emphasis on freedom at any cost. The 5 toddler will not thank you for a gleaming new playpen.

Advice: Take it easy, but take it
Avoid: Dangerous liaisons

6

6s are creative, logical and can be very kind. They see the beauty of things around them, and are mechanically minded. They love to gallivant around the town, up interesting alleys in the hope of finding something new. The worst thing you can do to a 6 is to drop in when his house is unusually untidy. They are so proud that they may well fib and say they've just been burgled. Devoted to committees, *causes célèbres* and home comforts, 6s can exhaust themselves with trivia and miss the big show. Children of a 6 can suffer from the energetic parent's expectations of them. The unwittingly pushy 6 may sour his or her offspring on the road to performance skills if he or she is not careful. 6s' desks will be littered with family snapshots: a way of expressing their pride in what they have created for the world.

Advice: Listen to others
Avoid: Stage mothering

7

A 7 has one foot off the planet, always analysing and explaining the unexplained. Lateral thinkers, they often find solutions when all hope has expired. They possess no patience with the workshy when operating positively and often work long hours themselves. The 7 is the initiated one, the teacher, the holder of information. When academic skill and intuition are vented healthily the 7 is a gold mine of wisdom and explorative thought patterns. When in crisis they prefer to withdraw and sort out their own worries. This withdrawal factor in their personalities can make them hypochondriacs, worrying that they might have some fatal illness, when in fact it is just a sniffle. They often walk alone in life and need time, space and masses of information to survive in peak condition.

Advice: Don't let yourself be hemmed in

Avoid: Isolation

8

8s are often victims of circumstance through no fault of their own, sometimes suffering through another's failure in business or emotion. Things happen to or around 8s. They rise to the challenge at the drop of a hat. 8 is the only time two circles appear in the chart. The top part of the 8 symbolises the spiritual side, the higher mind; the lower half the material side, the planet work. The 8 is a good person to be in a lifeboat with. They are resolute, calm, dependable and may want to get to shore to check their shares on the Dow Jones. Their strength is their greatest asset and they have a knack of being 'our man on the spot', giving eye-witness accounts of their experiences, whether exciting or painful. Pragmatic to the nth degree, the 8 gets through hell and high water, and through that pain, great learning is achieved.

Advice: Aspire

Avoid: Fear

9

Charming, debonair and caring, 9s are difficult to pin down yet give generously at all times. They do well in public life and the media but when operating negatively can drain unsuspecting others and become destroyers. The 9 is always, but always, on top of the invitation list and makes good dinner party company. The masters of small talk, they wheedle information out of others and have no hesitation when presenting new facts in passing them off as their own. Such is their love of the good life that they are often interested in antiques and have an eye for art. The 9 is known as the master of the grand gesture, and any gifts received from the beauty-loving 9 will be wrapped in a separate work of artistic merit.

Advice: Serve the needy
Avoid: Professional victims and users

10

10 is a master number which denotes a struggle before ultimate success. The 10 knows all about ships over-turning as they reach the safety of a port or luck running out just as they need it most. So near yet so far could be their motto or a major part of their life. This does not in any way mean the 10 is a loser, but it may mean that the carrier truly misused power as a 1 in a previous life or has chosen to learn the lesson of controlling his or her personal environment in a posi-tive way. 10s are not victims of failure, but witnesses to cause and effect. They are informed through vast experiences and gain the admiration of others when operating positively.

Advice: Stick with it
Avoid: Pigheadedness

11

A master number, 11 carries a special trump card of illuminated insight. The 11 carries a talent for enlightening others, healing rifts in relationships and gaining and accepting knowledge of the higher mind. 11s often walk a lonely road, and can find the restrictions that marriage and dependent relationships bring stifling. An 11 who discounts or ignores his or her spiritual leanings can lead a sorry and frustrating existence. They are here on an extra special or difficult mission and need to be aware that the simplest route is the most direct through any lifetime. The 11 gives the impression of being in a 'different space' and can be considered eccentric. Parents of an 11 child might worry about his or her solitary nature and are encouraged not to force the pace. 11s need a lot of space to work out the extra lesson and knowledge they carry.

Advice: Listen to your intuition

Avoid: The shady side of life

22

22 is known as the master builder in numerology, and with good reason. You were born with the potential for greatness in your lifetime, but the law of greatness has one demand, which is that you respect and appreciate its power. Your comprehension of life is colossal and your knowledge of many subjects wide. Like a double 11, 22s are interested in the workings of the occult and the higher mind as well as the city and stock exchange. They are inveterate chatterboxes and spouters, constantly transmitting what they have learned. Blessed or cursed with the fastidious 4's vibration (2 + 2 = 4), the 22 has the knack of spotting the rotten

apple in the barrel. They fare well in life when applying their insight and tenacity to the human cause. There is, however, a very serious downside to the 22 – a negative 22 is one of the worst human beings to encounter. Terror, manipulation and greed come easily to the erring 22.

Advice: Govern

Avoid: Smarm and duplicity

33

The most difficult number to carry. It is the number of martyrdom, unconditional love and caring. Very few people can vibrate at the full 33 level, and many choose to operate at the 3 + 3 = 6 vibration. 33s must guard against attracting lame ducks and cadgers because of their nurturing nature. They will be the first to be asked to carry a banner for a cause, and would be well advised to sit on their hands for five minutes before accepting. In short, don't fire the bullet for weak people. Children are drawn to 33s and benefit from being in their company. Caretakers of the planet is an apt title for the caring 33s, and often they will be found working with animals or wildlife organisation.

Advice: Don't be afraid to heal

Avoid: People who have no intention of getting well or living for themselves

THE GRID

This simple grid of nine squares will be the holder of all numbers for clarity, separation and analysis. The numbers go in the same boxes at all times. Number locations are highlighted below.

Please note that 0 has no place on the grid because it represents a lesson that has been learned in a previous life, but which will be useful in this life at some point.

3	6	9
2	5	8
1	4	7

Taking each figure of the birthdate separately, as we did when adding them up to find the life path number, position each digit in the relevant box. A 12/7/1965 birthdate would be placed as follows within the grid:

	6	9
2	5	
11		7

This is the first move in analysing a date of birth. The grid is your ally, your container from now on. It allows you to scan the pattern of the numbers you are working with through the horizontal and vertical planes, and through the trait lines, which we'll come to a little later on. They run north-south, east-west and diagonally right and left. This may seem a lot to take in initially, but it is easy to relate to if you remember that the whole picture is looking back at you from the page offering much information. Your eye will soon be able to scan the grid and assimilate the information.

On p.48 is the framework of the grid. The first lesson to learn about the grid is that it is made up of layers, vertically and horizontally. The first analysis to make is of the vertical planes, which pertain to the relationship between the *mother*, *father* and *self*. This gives an insight into the effect of the role modelling the carrier of the date of birth has chosen to learn from this lifetime's experiences. Note that if the child is adopted or lives with a guardian other than his or her natural mother or father this will still apply as we all learn generally from adults how to behave in society, whether the lesson is positive or negative.

We all have a feminine side and a masculine side, and this makes up the core, the self. The second overall analysis is of how the numbers relate in each plane of information. The feminine side overlays the mother, the self overlays the individual and the masculine side over-lays the father.

The Grid Framework and Planes
As well as a grid to hold the numbers we have an added framework of explanation through the meaning of the planes – vertical and horizontal – and the trait lines, which we will come to shortly.

Individual
Female *(Self)* **Male**
(Mother) *(Father)*

Thinking
(Logic)

Feeling
(Emotions)

Doing
*(Action and
Material Reward)*

THE MEANING OF NUMBERS AND MULTIPLE NUMBERS IN A DATE OF BIRTH

The number of identical numbers you have in your date of birth and name has special significance in analysing more deeply the characteristics which make up your personality. A general guideline is that the higher the multiple the more intense and stifling the vibration.

If, for example, your date of birth is 17/11/1944, then your multiples are: 4×1, 2×4, 1×9, 1×7.

Because of the rarity of a birthdate with five or more of the same number, I have given the meanings for up to four instances of the same number in any date of birth, apart from 1, for which a multiple of five is fairly common.

48

1

1 is the 'I', how you are in life and how you perceive your personal power.

1: Low self-esteem. You need to boost your self-esteem by realising that you beat millions of other sperms to claim this life in the womb. In short, your lesson is to realise that you have already won the hardest race you will ever have to run.

Special note: Treat yourself often, and treasure your gift of life by living it to the full.

11: Slightly competitive, but sensitive to harsh words from others. You need to be heard and must avoid bossy, insensitive people.

Special note: Excellent with a 4 or 7 in the trait line of materialism (see p.63).

111: Good sense of self-worth. You like to be the innovator and a helpful organiser. You have been encouraged by your mother or a significant female in your life.

Special note: On a chart with missing 5 gives a boost to self-esteem.

1111: Domineering, has to be right. You can be a show-off and a bit of a know-all, then wonder quite innocently why everyone is annoyed with you. You can suffer communication breakdowns because of a dominant, dismissive streak.

Special note: On a chart with multiple 7s frustration can lead to illness.

11111: Can be very difficult to live with, guilty of interfering in the lives of others and find living with themselves arduous. Their long-suffering friends need to be patient.

Special note: A 5 on the chart can reduce the tension of so many 1s.

2
The thinker and loyal friend. The worrier and the peacemaker.

2: Mulls things over, likes to consider all aspects before committing to an answer. You are a home-lover and loyal friend to have. You love to be of help.

Special note: Multiples of 8 on a chart can oppress the holder.

22: You live very much in the head, and can live in the 'I wish' world. A silent critic.

Special note: Act more often and make your wish come true.

222: Spends most of life proverbially standing on one leg, never moving forwards. You appear critical and often are.

Special note: You are unhappy if you don't and may be happy if you do. Try it.

2222: Possesses a built-in abort button which prevents good being felt in positive situations.

Special note: Learn the meaning of this sentence: I am a failure, I have tried and failed; it is also OK to fail.

3
Sensitive to the needs of others. Others may find them too light-hearted at times.

3: Sense of caring for others and the community. You will work unpaid or for low reward. You love happy endings and the fun things in life.

Special note: A good sense of purpose and knowing

what to do and just when is a plus when a 6 is on the head trait.

33: Puts others first but expects full recognition. You can be a touch martyrish. You must live life at your evolution rate and not rush into charity work too young.

Special note: Live each day as if it was your last and, you know something, that's the best anyone gets as a guarantee.

333: Tends to manipulate in personal relationships to suit him or herself, but is very good in legal situations. Often brilliant writers, they must convert the energy they invest in apathy to a purpose.

Special note: Talk it out and release the need to control outcomes.

3333: Rare, and just as well. Sensitive? Semtex! Isolation or walking alone through life can actually suit them very well.

Special note: We all need a crack at the limelight, so sit down and give us all a break!

4

Money needn't be a problem for long. Must have everything just so.

4: Money to be handled with caution during lifetime, whether in substantial or small amounts. Those with a single 4 in their chart can make a broth out of anything when money is tight.

Special note: Keep it tidy to win.

44: Possibility of a win or substantial windfall at some point in life, but what use would it be if you don't know how to spend it?

Special note: Money is a tool, not a burden.

444: A worker who will make his or her own way

through sheer endeavour. You have an extraordinary eagle eye and can find a jewel in a council tip. You live for the maxim 'If you want a job done well, then do it yourself.' Mean? 'Pop round for half a cup of coffee,' you might say.

Special note: Learn to delegate, and fairly. Even staff have private lives.

4444: Worry about never having enough security. Security equals possessions and a full larder. You love the supermarket at five minutes before closing time when 'reduced' labels are your turn-on.

Special note: Take a chance – it could open another door.

5

Lover of freedom, the seashore or country and liberal in love – sometimes too liberal for a partner or spouse's liking!

5: Generally a kind person who enjoys company, but at his or her own invitation. You are a good, reliable friend to have.

Special note: Treat me well and I'll respond accordingly.

55: Sociable, but tends to telephone too often for others' liking. You know the type. Half an hour about them, then they tell you they must go, and by the way, how are you? Click.

Special note: Learn to listen.

555: Charming, giddy and vivaciously bossy. You need lots of attention and tend to be a people-pleaser. You also choose high-rejection professions such as being an actor or astronaut.

Special note: Learn to treasure confidences, not broadcast them.

5555: A very rare type who are overtly daring and look for the ultimate thrills and spills, leaving family and friends puzzled or biting the skirting-board. They are capable of making irreparable mistakes.

Special note: You don't have to respond to every challenge.

6

Knowledge is power. Intelligent, creative, inquisitive and acquisitive. Loves committee work and Neighbourhood Watch.

6: Very creative. You could be a writer, painter, sculptor or designer. You might settle for being good at cartoons at school.

Special note: Sitting by the fire on a wet winter afternoon is heaven for 6.

66: Excellent with information and detail in the creative world. You might use this skill to design or assist others with their taste weaknesses.

Special note: Never scorn. Show others how, and reap the rewards for this skill.

666: Everything *must* match, including people. You are curious, nosy, interested; you need information. You want to know the name of the mother of the guy who designed Big Ben.

Special note: King Canute may have bequeathed you his stubbornness.

6666: Extremely logical. You have the destructive ability to ride roughshod over the heartfelt dreams of innocent others. You are quite secretive and can be accusatory, to your embarrassment. You are often very numerate. You're a good judge of character, but don't give enough praise, especially when it's due.

Special note: Live and let live.

7

Determined. Analyses for the universal Olympic team. Loves to teach others what they know.

7: Is the masculine number, the number of determination and dexterity. The 7 works long, isolated hours to succeed.

Special note: Play can be instructive too.

77: Determined verging on stubborn, often favouring isolation. You are the ultimate hobbyist. Relaxation is not a word in your vocabulary.

Special note: You are never alone, but developing in the way you have chosen.

777: Can be very headstrong. You don't know the meaning of the word can't. Spiritual and scientific knowledge has you as a catalyst. You're a good person in a storm, and there will be many storms: carriers often marry twice in their struggle to be understood.

Special note: Don't spend too long trying to pick up a superglued coin from the pavement. Move on!

7777: The pigheadedness of 4×7 can lead to unnecessary loss. Patience is a word they must learn to respect in order to placate their nervous disposition.

Special note: It is a rare and difficult road you have chosen but it has a purpose – don't give up.

8

Seekers of balance on the planet. They veer from extreme to extreme in character, great home-makers to victims of circumstance, through no fault of their own.

8: An 8 can experience some amazing events, some

good, some awful, but never dull. An 8 is a good boss to work for.

Special note: Expressing freely from the heart benefits the 8 carrier.

88: Witnesses of sadness in their lifetime; not always connected directly to themselves. They make excellent reporters by being 'our man on the spot'.

Special note: Don't demand unrealistic commitment from others.

888: Denotes a difficult section at some point in life, perhaps a loss through circumstances caused by other's failure. They are, however, masters at picking themselves up, dusting themselves down and starting over again.

Special note: Please show us lesser mortals how it's done.

8888: The saints of endurance in numerology. They are difficult to pin down for answers or commitment. They mean well, but sometimes cannot get their act together. 4×8 would be well advised to nurture other numbers in their chart to offset the burden of multiple 8s.

Special note: Concentrate more, don't allow others to hijack your life's script.

9
Good gut reactions to experiences. Needs the good life to survive in any form of contentment.

9: Makes you much harder on yourself and you can spend a lifetime looking for something that doesn't exist. Learn to bend with the opinion of others instead of snapping into submission.

Special note: Pride before a fall; illusion after a lie.

99: Highly intuitive. 2×9 have good gut reactions in decision-making but they have to learn that not everything in life has to be 100 per cent. They abhor untidiness and clothing which does not make a statement about them.

Special note: How long can you keep up this pressure on yourself?

999: Dismissive of fools. They can be grumpy and are at their best in the afternoons. Bad at making personal decisions, they are easily drawn into the conspiracy of paranoia.

Special note: Trust more in the process of life rather than the twist.

9999: Perfectionists with a dangerous habit of ignoring the mundane. You are advised that it is safe to live on the planet. Why? To develop!

Special note: Life is easy, it's the demands we make that are difficult.

TRAIT LINES

Shown on the following pages are the trait lines, which are fifteen vertical, horizontal and diagonal arrowed lines which give us much more information about the numbers we carry; an insight into our behaviour patterns and what we are learning from them. So far, there have been twelve in all, but from the millennium and after the year 2001 three more will be drawn to our attention. When a trait line is empty it indicates a potential for weakness; when it is full it is the potential for a strength. Always remember the two sides of the coin – positive operation and negative operation.

The arrows showing the trait lines, the numbers themselves, and how many numbers there are in each square should all be carefully considered. Too many numbers (for example, more than three) or too few (one or an empty square) denote an overpowering influence and a weakness respectively. Always keep the life path number in mind when analysing the trait lines. Many people have weak charts but a strong sense of purpose (life path) which can overcome obstacles.

The Line of Dependence/Independence
Example for birthdate 13/7/1972

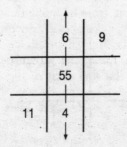

Example for birthdate 16/4/1955

The line of dependence in the first chart shows the individual's weakness as an independent single unit. This person is a good organiser and is very active but may seek to gain the approval or the guidance of others before committing himself. This person has to learn to congratulate himself and fill his own cup of happiness before he can fulfil the needs of others. Note the bookish/scholarly trait in the two 7s. After you have read and understood this section come back and see if you can spot his lines of organisation and movement.

The line of independence in the second chart cuts right through the individual plane and this one is full of numbers. This chart indicates a character who has had to work for everything he has wanted. See the weakness on the mother and father columns. A very strong chart, this, with a dramatic side in the plane of emotions.

The Line of Resolve/Indecision
Example for birthdate 5/3/1962

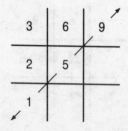

Example for birthdate 6/3/2022

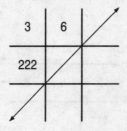

The line of resolve in the first chart shows an extremely determined and motivated person who, once she begins, will get the job done. This chart also has a fairly stable emotional side, too (the 2 and 5 in the emotions plane). Remember, a blank box is a weakness to be observed and strengthened this time round on the planet.

In the twenty-first century, new trait lines will become possible for the first time. For the date 6/3/2022 we have a new trait line of indecision, which is the opposite of the full trait line of resolve. I feel that this could be a time of non-aggression, although with all the 2s it could also be a time of worry.

Notice that, like life, numerology is evolving all the time.

The Line of Emotional Stability/Over-Sensitivity
Example for birthdate 18/5/1921

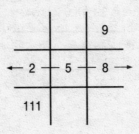

Example for birthdate 19/6/1937

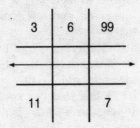

The first chart shows someone who is warm, loving and resourceful, with a strong line of resolve (find that one yourself, please). The 2, 5 and 8 complete the emotions plane and indicate the carrier's potential to find true happiness and contentment during this lifetime. The three 1s also indicate a good sense of self given by the mother/female coupled with the 9 and 8 on the father/male side of the chart. This child has a good set of role models.

The second chart shows a lesson to be learned concerning matters of the heart and emotions. This person may suffer shyness and restrictions in attracting a partner. He must learn to follow his heart and speak proudly from feelings as well as logic. Once you have learned the trait lines, find the line of logic on this chart.

The Line of Logic/Poor Recall
Example for birthdate 16/5/1923

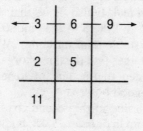

Example for birthdate 17/2/1888

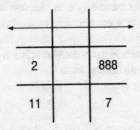

The first chart indicates that the carrier has the potential to possess the intellect of the academic and will choose to analyse first, then feel. It also shows that she is emotionally stable (the 2 and the 5 in the emotions plane show that she is more stable than unstable). When you have analysed the trait lines find the line of organisation, skills which, when added to the line of logic, indicate the potential to be a good boss.

So far, the trait line in the second chart has appeared only for people born in or before 1888, but will occur again for those born from the year 2000 onwards. As we come to analyse those born in the 21st century the number of people with a blank column of logic (top line) will multiply considerably. It is to be hoped that the species begins acting as humans instead of just talking about it logistically. To me this configuration suggests that we will be leading a peaceful and less stressful lifestyle and living more from the heart. On the negative side it could express extinction, but that is not an idea I invest in. If we look at history before 1888 there were scholars and academics, but viewed on a large scale there was a lot more manual labour than cerebral activity in the Industrial Revolution. Remember, to the Third World westerners are a dubiously 'refined' few, and as for extinction – well, the world didn't come to an end before 1888 when the line of logic was poor.

The Line of Materialism/Non-Materialism
Example for birthdate 3/5/1947

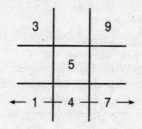

Example for birthdate 3/6/2020

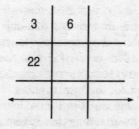

The line of materialism indicates an inclination towards

money and chattels and the carrier will be drawn towards the materialistic side of life. He may also show excellent saving skills when younger and hurt more than most when burgled – whether he is massively insured or not.

After the year 2001 we will have a new trait line of non-materialism. This may bring a trait in our evolution where, as the example grid for birthdate 3/6/2020 shows you, we are operating from the plain of emotion.

The Line of Organisation
Example for birthdate 17/3/1992

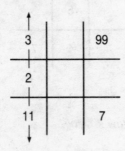

The line of organisation shows that the carrier is prepared to put up or shut up. She loves to get things moving and is well motivated. Such carriers are often found in voluntary services or activities which need attention to detail for smooth running. Once you have learned the trait lines look out for the line of dependence in this chart and, by attaching this information to the line of organisation, note the struggle within the chart. This is someone who gets on with it even though she is not always sure at times.

Until the year 4000, an empty trait line of disorganisation will be impossible because of the presence of the 1 in the 20th century, the 2 in the 21st century and the 3 in the 22nd century.

The Line of Movement/Inertia
Example for birthdate 15/3/1978

Example for birthdate 2/2/2001

In the first chart we have a person who prefers to be on the move and always up and doing. This shows in the line of movement. A person with this chart will be inventive and possess a love of travel, especially with the 8 in his emotions plane. Remember to look at the whole picture: up, down and across the trait lines; and the planes: Mother, Individual, Father etc. Spotted the line of resolve yet? Good!

For the birthdate 2/2/2001 we have the new trait line of inertia. This may bring an era when we stay at home, and everything is done for us, perhaps cars themselves will chauffeur those of us who choose to go out to work. Robot world?

The Line of Self-Esteem/Cynicism
Example for birthdate 13/12/1957

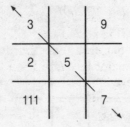

Example for birthdate 14/6/1982

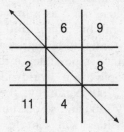

The first chart shows a marvellous sense of self-worth – the line of self-esteem – and a very determined streak (the latter is for you to find). If you check your multiple numbers in a chart section you will generally find that the carrier has a very good sense of humour too (the two 3s).

The second chart shows the subject to be creative in the written word (the 6 and the 2), but the line of cynicism prevents her from experimenting too much. This person has a major lesson to learn this time round and that is to believe in herself and to trust more in the process of life. The 2 and 8 in her emotions plane hint at many experiences of love. 8 is travel experience and change, 2 is helping or diplomacy when operating positively – when not, it is the opposite.

My last word on trait lines is *always remember your multiple numbers in a chart* when reading a grid, and the life path number of the person being analysed.

As a matter of interest, a spectacular numerological

configuration occurs again after the millennium. We lose the 9 as a foundation number in the grid and after the year 2200 we lose the 1 as a foundation number. This gives us new trait line configurations – some lines will have a new potential to be empty and in others an empty trait line will be impossible for the first time – as there will be people born worldwide on 2/2/2222, 22/2/2222 or 22/2/2200. Naturally, there will also be people born on 1/9/2200 and so on, but a new generation of human beings will vibrate at a 2 and 1 foundation for the first hundred years, and 22 in the second hundred, just as the population who entered the 20th century vibrated to a 1 and a 9 foundation. The exciting part is that this time many of us will see in the millennium and those of you who are new numerologists will, I hope, be observers of this changeover. Look below. Quite a grid, isn't it?

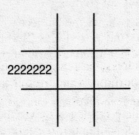

DATE OF BIRTH SCAN
As well as analysing the digits which make up a date of birth, you also need to know how to analyse the date in three sections.

The date of birth 27/8/1977, for example, shows us the following:

27 is the first fact about the carrier. The day of birth is the immediate influence to which the carrier responds. The gut reaction on a day-to-day basis.

8 is the second, the middle-distance influence, governs the overall instinct; the pivot, if you like, which balances the date of birth. Its influence gives a more long-term view of the carrier's behaviour.

1977 is the long-term vibration, the influence which runs throughout the carrier's lifetime. It is a very important influence in that it is the universal year number the carrier is born into. This is the number which keeps the carrier anchored to earth's current vibration. Earth is constantly moving and we join her cycle, her process, and leave it without her stopping.

With the date of birth 27/8/1977, reduce each section thus: 27 (2 + 7 = 9) − 8 − 1977 (1 + 9 + 7 + 7 = 24; 2 + 4 = 6). (If the result is a master number, do not reduce it further.) For the purpose of the overall assessment, this date of birth now reads: 9/8/6.

9 is the immediate influence or vibration on a daily basis. 8 is the middle influence, the referee, and 6 is the vibration which recurs throughout the carrier's lifetime.

THE MEANINGS OF DAY, MONTH AND YEAR OF BIRTH INFLUENCES
Each number applies to the day, month or year influences
  1: Leadership qualities which must be acknowledged.

2: A need to keep the peace and to serve others.

3: Humour in most things, and the care of others without being manipulated.

4: The need for order and precision. Business-minded.

5: The influence of music, theatre and a heightened sense of drama.

6: Information is power and the fruits it yields.

7: A need for space and learning.

8: Balance, power and comfort.

9: Catalysing of people, facts, and universal power.

10: Struggle before the trophy.

11: Development of psychic ability, pursuit of truth and kindness.

22: The use of power in its most constructive form. Without being tempted.

33: The healer and missionary on a bumpy but worthwhile road.

PERSONAL YEARS

The personal year is the year you are currently in during the continual nine-year cycle of numerological growth within your lifetime. When we know our personal year and its significance, we are able to plan for our future. The guideline of the personal year is to give yourself twelve months' progress through learning which will enhance the lessons of the year before and prepare the path for the following one.

Your personal year is calculated by replacing the birth year by the year number of your last birthday. Personal years operate from birthday to birthday, *not* from 1 January to 31 December. For example, if your birthdate is 9 August 1945, and the year of your last birthday is

1994, replace the 1945 with 1994 and reduce to a single digit: 9/8/1994: $9 + 8 + 1 + 9 + 9 + 4 = 40$; $4 + 0 = 4$. Remember that master numbers – 10, 11, 22 and 33 – do not reduce, so if your birthday is 6 October and the last one was in 1993, your personal year is 11: $5 + 1 + 0 + 1 + 9 + 9 + 4 = 29$; $2 + 9 = 11$.

The Meaning and Potential of the Personal Years

1

The 1 year is about new beginnings, making changes in the way you do things – perhaps thinking about moving house or changing jobs – letting go of the old ways. It's a time when you could be forgiven for thinking that nothing is happening, but remember, a beautiful flower is only a seed in the beginning.

Advice: Wakey, wakey! Time to stretch yourself again
Avoid: Apathy and postponing

2

The 2 year is about partnerships and unions, in both personal and business relationships. On the negative side, it's also a year when you are slightly vulnerable emotionally, so watch out for some emotional aerobics. Even so, generally it's a year to nurture optimism.

Advice: Trust in life
Avoid: Worrying too much

3

The 3 year is about creativity and using energies wisely. It's a year for taking and making time for yourself physically and mentally, perhaps thinking about starting that degree course, or joining the gym. Not a great time to make drastic change, but having fun, yes. Nurture yourself.

Advice: Lay down the burden and live a little

Avoid: Dangerous exploits

4

The 4 year is about bringing order into your life, a time to realise that you are the captain of your ship. Succeed with that diet, trim the sails to set your course, extend your home. 4 is a year of building and making a workable framework within which to live.

Advice: Sort it out, and fast

Avoid: Exhaustion

5

The 5 year is a year of travel and expansion. If you want to change your annual holidays from Bournemouth to Bolivia, then this is the year to make the move. In any business dealings in this year, be mindful of small print which could tie you unnecessarily.

Advice: Respect your freedom

Avoid: Restrictive relationships

6

The 6 year is a year of emotional highs. Family comes to the fore, and on the home front it's a year of meeting and enjoying home comforts. You could be extending your home or your family through a birth or a wedding. It's a time of giving. Artistic, business and creative ventures are pretty inspired. It is a year in which feelings are to the fore.

Advice: New ideas and power

Avoid: Narcissism and exploitation

7

The 7 year is a time of getting to know your true self. It's the year of coming to terms with who and why you are. It can be a year of painful recognition: perhaps you've been doing things the hard way. The 7 year is about making sure that what you're longing for is what you really want. It does us good to stop and take stock every now and again. Books can show you where to look, but experience is the teacher.

Advice: Look deep inside to the true you
Avoid: Pedantry and stinginess

8

The 8 year is a year of achievement and getting there. Money could be better this year and next year, more so than it has for the last couple of years. The benefits of your efforts may not bear fruit until next year, but at least you have notched up the learning.

Advice: Hold out your arms and catch what you need
Avoid: Self-inflicted loneliness

9

In the 9 year you reap what you have sown. It is a time of harvesting and rewards. The harvest can be financial or emotional. It's a year when you can call in all your favours and resources; a time of disposing of anything which has outstayed its welcome. It may also bring painful separations.

Advice: A time of reality and making space for the new
Avoid: Emotional blackmail

10

There is nothing that will convince you that the 10 year will come up trumps in the end, but I'm going to say it anyway. This year is about making it after a struggle and a half. The short-cut is to use something from the old ways, an ancient skill or ancient knowledge, to resolve, plough through or negotiate the outcome you want.

Advice: Don't step off the wheel of fortune

Avoid: People who might persuade you to give up

11

The 11 year is about the higher mind, intuition, gaining valuable insight into yourself and enlightening others; a year of finding peace of mind in areas of your life which are in need of it. This year gives you another unique chance to re-evaluate yourself. It's a time of understanding yourself and others through the valuable illuminated vibration of the 11 year. You may experience many valuable shifts in the way you live your life.

Advice: Be open to universal suggestion and your inner voice messages

Avoid: Vagueness and self-denial

22

This is a master number builder year. It's a special year of consolidating the foundation of what you know and who you are. The 22 year is a time of career, business and gaining promotion within large corporations. Care is needed in abundance when reading the small print in legal documents or contractual arrangements, from the insurance guarantee on your new washing machine to the employment package of your new job. A 22 year is

the year to consolidate any long-term projections.
Advice: Don't sit up the cul-de-sac waiting for success; be at the corner to guide it in
Avoid: Picking up coins when the paper money is flying around

33

The master number 33 year is a very rare year in that it is applicable to very few people as a full 33 vibration. It is a year of caring, one in which you may consider devoting yourself to working for humanitarian causes such as nursing, training for some kind of therapy or launching a community project. You would be well advised to do some soul-searching into why you want to pursue this kind of commitment before embarking upon it. Sometimes it is more prudent to reduce the 33 to the more comfortable 6 vibration, as a 33 year can be a painfully heavy one to carry through. People in this personal year must take care to avoid people who make the bullets and expect the 33 to fire the gun.
Advice: Create new boundaries within which to live
Avoid: Liars, cheats and false flattery

PERSONAL MONTHS
A personal month indicates the potential for understanding during any given month the most harmonious vibrations available. A personal month calculation is used either personally or in the business world to choose the most advantageous vibration.

The great thing about a personal month is that you have between twenty-eight and thirty-one days in which to maximise the potential of that particular month. During the period you can maximise the potential of the day number and add that to your forward planner. Take a look at nature – she doesn't make a heatwave in Switzerland in January. In nature spring, summer, autumn and winter have a pattern, a vibration, a purpose, and so does numerology.

A personal month is reached by adding your current personal year to the month whose potential you want to know and reducing the figure as appropriate (January is month 1 and December month 12). Remember that the personal year is the day + the month + the year of your last birthday, not your birth year.

So if the personal year is 9 and the month you wish to know about is March, the third month of the year, then the calculation is: 9 + 3 = 12; 1 + 2 = 3.

The Meaning and Potential of the Personal Months

A 1 month: The month when the vibration is for making major changes or taking chances on the new. A good time to open a new business or do things in a more constructive way.

A 2 month: Consolidate any new changes and allow family matters to come to the fore. It is also a time for reading the small print and dotting the 'i's and crossing the 't's.

A 3 month: A month when burdens ease. It provides an opportunity to fall in love or have an affair – but above all be careful that the fun does not cost you for years to come.

A 4 month: Leaves you with no time to rest on your laurels. Up off the sofa and busy, busy, busy. This is an excellent month for renovating or repairing. What you have started you can finish now.

A 5 month: A time of surprises, some good, some not so

good. During a 5 month gain more by operating instinctively rather than logically or emotionally.

A 6 month: This can be a testing time and your loyalty might be strained more than any other characteristic. Domesticity is the keynote and intimate relationships are spotlighted.

A 7 month: This vibration helps you to add to your skills through study or seeking answers to long-standing questions. It is a most important rest stop before the success vibration of the 8 month.

An 8 month: Is a welcome vibration of possibility at its highest. Imagine yourself in a lift going to the top floor of a very important building to receive a reward, an accolade or promotion and you'll understand the 8 vibration.

A 9 month: Offers peace, harmony and a bringing together of situations, people or information. It may not seem very comfortable in the short term, but the long-term effects of this month rid you of exhausting, time-wasting and draining patterns.

A master number 10 month: Allows you extra time to activate personal power, your strength and your daring side. Usually after the tenth or eleventh day of a 10 month the carrier will experience a powerful surge in ability and energy which can carry him or her to success.

A master number 11 month: gives an extra boost to the extra-sensory perception skills of the carrier. A heightened state of awareness is usually noticeable during the 11 vibration, and using this awareness can give you a substantial advantage over others in a purchase, job application or point of order.

PERSONAL DAYS

Personal days are an analysis of a twenty-four-hour period. Business personnel using numerology are encouraged by the potential of each hour, day, month, year and indeed moment. In one particular business reading I gave some years ago I suggested changing the meeting from a Friday, which was a 4 day for the client, to the following Tuesday, which was an 8 day. He duly did this, after much effort, and on the Monday evening documents came to light which pointed to a chaotic and fraudulent scam by one of his departing partners. By adhering to a fundamental rule of numerology – never force it, bend with it – he saved his corporation some serious money. I used the company's 'date of birth' – the date it was lodged at Companies House – the client's date of birth, and through personnel information the date of birth of the would-be fraudster. By cross-referencing the life paths of all three I could deduce a pattern of possibilities and probabilities which was eventually borne out. Don't sit in awe or disbelief at this – try it! I had to start somewhere too.

A personal day is calculated by adding the day and the month in question to the current *personal year* (i.e. the actual number arrived at, not the components of the birthday year). So if the day in question is 7/9/1944, and your personal year is a 9 year, add the day and the month (7 and 9), plus 9, and reduce to a single digit: $7 + 9 + 9 = 25; 2 + 5 = 7$.

You can also calculate the potential of a personal hour: add the day, month, hour in question and personal year.

The Meaning and Potential of the Personal Days

A 1 day: Opens up your daring streak and your ability to be you at all costs. It is a doing day right up until the clock strikes midnight. Selling the house or car? Divorcing? Today's the day!

A 2 day: A very personal day of tranquillity and flowing with the tide of contentment. Don't take the bait. Home is where the heart is and today's the day. Take the day off with your partner, have a romantic lunch and make love.

A 3 day: Spontaneous action and laughter. The gut reaction is your teacher today. Be available to life and its surprises, steer clear of gossips and do not do others' dirty work.

A 4 day: See your accountant and be nice to him or her. If it's your bank manager get to the point and don't take no for an answer – remember, the bank works for you. A good day for car repairs, testing for your pilot's licence, enrolling your child at Eton.

A 5 day: The hills are alive and so are you. Respect your freedom and truth. Speak from the heart, as you would prefer to be spoken to, and enjoy the rainbow effect of today's vibration.

A 6 day: The lawyer's and pragmatist's twenty-four hours. A good day to negotiate your parking fines, apply for planning permission, see your publisher. Committees get things passed today.

A 7 day: An information vibration and success in the teaching professions. Share gossip, inform and fill your memory banks with data. Back up all computer work. Spiritual insight is available to those who ask.

An 8 day: When the early bird catches the worm and compliments abound. Tie the knot, sign the documents and pat yourself on the back for being you.

A 9 day: Deal with and dispatch problems to their proper place. Slam down the phone on time-wasters and clear out your negative thoughts.

A 10 day: Unforeseen circumstances place a block of hurdles in front of you today. This understood, you almost have to let the gremlins wear themselves out and prepare to take the tape a few hours later than planned.

An 11 day: The kind of day when you wake up and just know you've got the answer before the problem has even surfaced. Automatic pilot works well. Listen to your gut reaction as well as your logic.

A 22 day: An excellent day for corporate deals, take-overs, successful interviews or legal wrangles. Providing you have told the truth in all matters the sky's the limit for windfalls, or for being in the right place at the right time.

A 33 day: A good day for giving apologies or receiving them. Donate blood or visit someone in hospital – you're in demand as a soother of fevered brows again!

PEOPLE WITH IDENTICAL DATES OF BIRTH

Now let's settle this question once and for all. Yes, there are people with identical birthdates – twins, friends, cousins, strangers. These people will show similar traits to their same-date peers but, except in the case of a twin, triplet, sextuplet or so on, they will not have the same parents' or siblings' numbers to learn from or relate to. That makes them very different from same-date-of-birth peers. We are not that complicated as a species – anyone who travels will tell you that. We have regional or cultural habits, but in any culture it all comes down to love, happiness, education, wealth and health, and how we cope with life's contrasts in the learning process. With twins there is an interesting way to analyse the life path in greater depth where we know the time of birth. First, let's see how the average numerologist would analyse the date of birth of twins.

Twin Girls Born 17/5/1976

	6	9
	5	
11		77

It is simple to gain further information by constructing a 'minutes' grid and adding the numbers of the minutes to the respective grids.

Twin 1 Grid

Twin 1 born at 11.14 p.m. on 17/5/1976

	6	9
	5	
11111	4	77

Twin 2 Grid

Twin 2 born at 11.22 p.m. on 17/5/1976

	6	9
22	5	
1111		77

With the extended information of the trait lines analyses, you will be able to see that Twin 1 shows more individualistic traits, and seeks independence, while the five 1s make her a bit quick with her tongue. Twin 2 is more prone to worrying because of the two 2s on her plane of emotions, but she is quite balanced, with a minimum of two numbers in each trait line. Numbers are always there to give us answers.

CUSP LIFE PATH NUMBERS

Something I have noticed emerging through the years in numerology is the cusp factor in the life paths of people born between approximately 11.30 p.m. and 12.30 a.m. For example, someone born at 11.57 p.m. on 25 May 1959 will have begun adjusting to life on 26 May. I have found that there will be a mixture of both days' vibrations shown in the person's life path number. One such client, a man born at 12.49 a.m. on 10 June 1950, had all the potential of the master number 22 life path – executive position, beautiful home, wife and children – and yet a reckless streak from the 3 life path contained within the 9 June 1950 had left him with his life in tatters through dangerous spontaneous actions on several occasions in his life with women and allowing his time to be hijacked by duplicitous people. Had this lifestyle suited him emotionally he would have had no problem, but he came off worst every time. My advice to him was literally to consult both life path numbers and take more care than most in sifting through any potential for error, thus continuing to remind himself of the pattern he'd unwittingly formed through the negative influence of a 3 vibration. This method of using the time of birth as well as the date of birth is useful when a life path number does not suit the character being analysed.

RESERVOIR NUMBERS

The reservoir numbers are number vibrations which hold keys to success in our previous life. How many times do we hear 'If only I knew what I was good at'? Well, there is no excuse: numerology offers that answer too. Reservoir numbers allow us to draw enormous untapped strength in times of crisis.

A reservoir number is a major lesson you learned well in a past life, with which you start this life's lessons. The future you have to learn, but the past gives you a helping start with this number.

So the reservoir number is a credit to enhance the numbers this time round. It is found by subtracting the life path number from 9. A life path 6 subtracted from 9 would give the reservoir number 3. The carrier may well bring joy into this lifetime with a natural caring streak. If your life path number is 9, you do not have a reservoir number ($9 - 9 = 0$). You have completed a 9 life cycle of learning. Hence the completion power of 0. People with the master numbers of 10, 11, 22 or 33 should subtract 9 from 10, 11, 22 or 33 and reduce to a single figure. For example, $10 - 9 = 1$. $11 - 9 = 2$. $22 - 9 = 13$; $1 + 3 = 4$. $33 - 9 = 24$; $2 + 4 = 6$.

This subtraction always gives you the same number as you would carry if you reduced your master number for your life path. For example, master number 11 reduces to 2 ($1 + 1 = 2$) and $11 - 9 = 2$; 22 reduces to 4 and $22 - 9 = 13$; $1 + 3 = 4$, and so on.

So during the years I have been a numerologist I have become more convinced that the reservoir number is a previous skill which is available without reducing the master number to a single digit, proving that the carrier has a chance to operate at a reduced or more comfortable level. I am convinced that it allows the lesser vibration of the master number to have been learned before coming through to this vibration of master number.

The Meaning and Potential of the Reservoir Numbers

1: You have a natural ability in leadership challenges to hand and a knack for seizing and making the most of the moment.

2: You learned to nurture in a past life and may be very homely and loving. You also have the peace-making skills of a top diplomat. You are trustworthy and a loyal employee and friend.

3: Cheering up others is a natural skill of yours. You have learned that swift action gets results. You have also learned about the female side of duplicity. You are easily and naturally inspired.

4: Finance has been a learning curve in a past life and you are better equipped to enjoy money instead of hoarding it for a rainy day. You are instinctively tidy, direct and find pleasure in order.

5: Freedom has been a learning curve for you, and you know this time how to respect it. You now know you can't please everybody, and neither should you. Others may have difficulty in trying to ensnare you into a restricting relationship. You find it easy to make and relate to friends.

6: You may have been a painter, sculptor or writer last time, draw (ouch!) on that skill now if you desire to be creative. You may be naturally gifted. Others are curious about your benevolence and feel warmed by your kind gestures.

7: You may have been a monk, teacher or priest in a past incarnation and may find solitude or deep thought quite a natural state. Applying knowledge of that wisdom to the now should be quite easy for you. You may also be close to your parish priest or vicar.

8: Your psychic ability may have cost you dear in the past but now you can witness life in freedom. The memory of practical skills the RN 8 holds still stands you in good stead and your coordination skills are good. Your level-headed approach may have shown very early in your childhood.

PINNACLES

The pinnacles, or 'peeks' are four years in our lives when we have an opportunity to pause just long enough to take a peek at the whole picture, to reassess our boundaries and how we are coping with our script so far; a bit like four spot-checks. The pinnacles are the motorway filling stations where you can pull in, fill with fuel and check the vehicle as well as feed the body and tend to basic needs.

The pinnacles must always be analysed in conjunction with your life path and ability numbers, and they most definitely do not stop and start on the stroke of midnight on the calculated date. Because there are only four of them they can build up before the pinnacle year, or begin to be noticed a bit into the pinnacle year.

Remember, in numerology you look at the whole picture. None of this she's a 5 life path so she must be . . . We don't deal in trailers in this book – it's the big picture or back to the drawing-board.

You calculate the pinnacles like this:

Write down the reduced totals of your month, day and year:

15/6/1961 = 6 + 6 + 8

Now add together the day and the month and reduce to single digit:

6 + 6 = 3
This is your first pinnacle

Add together the day and year and reduce to a single digit:

6 + 8 = 14; 1 + 4 = 5
This is your second pinnacle

Add together your first and second pinnacles and reduce to a single digit:

3 + 5 = 8
This is your third pinnacle

Add together your month and year and reduce to a single digit:

6 + 8 = 14; 1 + 4 = 5
This is your fourth pinnacle.

The Ages of Assessment

These are the ages when the effects of the pinnacles will be felt. Numerology recognises the number 36 as a collective age of maturity (it is derived simply from multiplying together the four nine-year life cycles). Freud states that around thirty-five or forty we achieve insight after our journey through life; it's sometimes called a mid-life crisis; I consider it a time to pause and reflect on the journey we have made and to assess whether there are any changes to be made which could enhance your life. To find your first pinnacle age assessment subtract the reduced number of your life path from 36 to reach your personal age of maturity. For example, 15/6/1962 = 30; 3 + 0 = 3. 36 − 3 = 33.

So 33 is the first pinnacle age assessment in this example, the first year of maturity when you are ready to assess what's gone before and how you've progressed. We all know people who mature faster or slower than others. Numerology is able to assess this progress.

As an extra exercise, subtract 9 from your first pinnacle age assessment and work back to your childhood through the nine-year cycles. You'll be surprised what you can pinpoint from memory. Remember, the life cycle of numerology is nine years. To find the second, third and fourth pinnacles, just add 9 to the first age of assessment. In our example, the second pinnacle would be 42 (33 + 9); third pinnacle 51 and the fourth pinnacle 60.

The fourth pinnacle lasts the rest of your life and gives you the opportunity to bring to fruition the effects of your life path journey. Rather than think of the later years as the departure lounge of life, consider them a perfect time to use retirement or the decelerating period to do what you wish you'd done before: travel; study; learn to be a potter, painter or candlestick maker; stop to watch the planet evolve. Consider the effects of the lessons you have or haven't learned.

The Pinnacles Ready Reckoner

This table enables you to find your pinnacle years at a glance. Look up your life path number in the left-hand column. The four relevant ages of assessment are given on the right.

Life path no.	Age at peak			
	1	2	3	4
1	35	44	53	62
2	34	43	52	61
3	33	42	51	60
4	32	41	50	59
5	31	40	49	58
6	30	39	48	57
7	29	38	47	56
8	28	37	46	55
9	27	36	45	54
10	26	35	44	53
29/11	25	34	43	52
22/4	32	41	50	59
33/6	30	39	48	57

The Meaning of Each Pinnacle

1
Leadership and going it alone

When 1 is a first pinnacle: The carrier could be forgiven for feeling all at sea. Even though it's a great time for fresh approaches, this is a time of learning that the L-plates are off and that the part of you which knew it all knows not enough. It may also be a period in which you have no choice but to shake off debilitating individuals whose emotional pain affects you.

When 1 is a second pinnacle: A settling-in period or a coming home can be felt through extended effort and a bit of daring. This can be a magical time of allowing the emotional desires and expressions free rein and reaping the harvest.

When 1 is a fourth pinnacle: The word 'chaos' must be acknowledged, then dealt with. Ambition tempered with truth is a prime option during this pinnacle. Promotion is possible providing the chaos potential of the negative 4 pinnacle is overcome.

2

Relationships, pairing and following your heart

When 2 is a first pinnacle: Frustrations or restrictions abound. The learning curve of this pinnacle is to be individual at all early costs. Others will ruffle their feathers and crow but stand firm. There is a potential for emotional blackmail, whether by family or a peer. Don't take the bait.

When 2 is a second pinnacle: Self-esteem will be stretched if the lessons of the first pinnacle have been ignored or delayed. The position of others in life must not be used as an excuse for failing to live up to your own dreams, schemes and desires. This is a prime period of self-recognition in the contentment stakes.

When 2 is a fourth pinnacle: The vibration is one of energetic eccentricity in old age and an understanding through preparing for comfort in the later years, both emotionally and financially.

3

Lightheartedness, creative reward and potential caring

When 3 is a first pinnacle: A vibration of coordinated eyes, head, hands and feet. This encompasses the arts as a whole and the ability to move into that sphere in a substantial way. However, the scattiness of the 3 is always there and having five jobs and no time to spend the spoils is no reward at all. A sense of proportion is recommended during this phase, and on reflection the carrier may be in a position to recognise this period as a fractious experience. It is never too late to learn from that lesson, and if the situation has a habit of repeating itself the carrier is able to understand through numerology how to make adjustments to break the pattern.

When 3 is a second pinnacle: The universal message of working to live instead of living to work is the learning curve. The potential for the big time is good during this phase, but this is a vibration when the potential to fasten a brick necklace around one's over-mortgaged neck is rife: flash homes and outward appearances of material success are marvellous, but not at the cost of family, health and broadening experience. Make time for fun.

When 3 is a fourth pinnacle: This can make the carrier a tyrant of a boss, parent or colleague. A time to assess if the payoff is worth the energy extended. Health problems could be symptomatic of failure to widen the lifestyle further than material gain.

4
Construction and order
When 4 is a first pinnacle: The emphasis is on a feeling of having to go it alone or provide for others or the self at an early age. With the 4 first pinnacle the carrier is usually not afraid of hard work and long hours.

When 4 is a second pinnacle: The health of the carrier is to be watched if the first pinnacle was carried out in full. The need for relaxation away from the ambition arena is the learning curve, and the carrier is also reminded that success does not equal hard work or restriction – success is for enjoying.

When 4 is a fourth pinnacle: The activity levels are high with the potential for the carrier's time to be taken up with the needs of others. This could be personal, or the flush of a late and new business venture commanding attention.

5

Freedom and risk

When 5 is a first pinnacle: The freedom-loving urge can cause uproar, loss and danger at times. Change is marvellous, but change for the sake of it or because it's on offer can lead to roots not having time to settle. It is, however, a period of intuitive urges and when the spiritual and spirited side is constructively adventurous the rewards are superb.

When 5 is a second pinnacle: The adventures of the flying 5 are both recognised and rewarding. This is the drama period and, taking it literally, music, theatre or writing may appeal to the expressiveness of the 5 vibration. Adventures must be well thought out in this period of a life path.

When 5 is a fourth pinnacle: The need for harmony in experiences is great. This is a period of bonding or gratitude for the support of others, either emotionally or practically.

6

Family and duty

When 6 is a first pinnacle: The vibration has the potential for guilt or rushing things. Volunteering for restricting committee work as a way to power or taking responsibility for events that took two to tango must be thought out in the long term instead of being acted on immediately. The moral of the vibration is don't bite off more than you can chew. What you think you want now may not be what you want in five years' time.

When 6 is a second pinnacle: The lesson is one of creative expression and the home is an attraction at this time. Nesting is the keyword: the desire to put down roots is strong. The need to be established and recognised is to the fore.

When 6 is a fourth pinnacle: A harmonious family and community life is indicated. Even in times of struggle a good family is hard to beat.

7
Analysis and contemplation

When 7 is a first pinnacle: The road to the answer can be nerve-racking and only you can get it right. You are a bit like an ice-skating champion: it's your time on the ice and you've got to get it right.

When the 7 is a second or third pinnacle: The emphasis is on learning, learning and learning, and the ability to convert this into a career or business. Your confidence is your best ally, and the will to succeed is essential.

When 7 is a fourth pinnacle: It may draw you to spiritual and religious questions which could need commitment if you are to gain the best of the knowledge analysed.

8
Getting there, success and accolades

When 8 is a first pinnacle: Gordon Gekko is your middle name. Ambition is your destination, and there is ample use of your wheeler-dealer streak.

When 8 is a second pinnacle: Legal matters, share dealings and capital gains are the focus providing motivation is there. There is no such thing as a free fortune, so there's only one way you're going to get it – by taking responsibility for it.

When 8 is a third pinnacle: Health is another major consideration. Money is a great servant but a bad master.

When 8 is a fourth pinnacle: Your entry into the grey army – the exclusive club for those who never retyre, but simply retread – is guaranteed. You're a wise old budgie in this phase.

9
Preparing for expansion and moving on

When 9 is a first pinnacle: Membership of the boy scouts or girl guides appeal to the giving 9 and the uniform nature of the first phase. Dominant parents are also a bone of contention in this phase.

When 9 is a second pinnacle: Restriction in emotional expression may manifest itself as shyness or awkwardness with the opposite sex. Lead on, Macduff, for there is nothing like the fun of catching up for the late developer.

When 9 is a third pinnacle: Early marriage and an early divorce may end this phase of searching for love, success and the next phase of your script.

When 9 is a fourth pinnacle: It may surprise the carrier. The fruit of the loom is available providing depression is curbed throughout the heavy learning phase.

10
Success against all odds

When 10 is a first pinnacle: The emphasis is on clearing the hurdles for success through learning to use power properly.

When 10 is a second pinnacle: Much work must be done in keeping a rational perspective in self-esteem and avoiding bullying individuals.

When 10 is a third pinnacle: It's make or break time for the potential of the 10 as a third pinnacle. Keep assessing boundaries and looking for and enjoying new avenues in which to excel.

When 10 is a fourth pinnacle: You may be making the finishing touches to your round-the-world yacht, or your insurance policy may just have matured. Whatever, you are on a roller-coaster ride to many new experiences and you might just have acquired the courage to let your hair down a bit.

11

Insight, illumination, truth, interpretation

When 11 is a first pinnacle: The carrier will be in the first cycle of life. The child should be encouraged to express his or her spiritual side through Sunday school or helper-oriented clubs. Listen to the feelings and forecasts of the highly intuitive 11 child: 11s are involved in the human cause from their day of birth and must be respected for their gentle ways and need for tranquillity.

When 11 is a 2nd pinnacle: It affords recognition of and a *laissez faire* attitude towards material life. During this phase the carrier's choice of partner is more crucial, as he or she will need to be understanding and non-clinging in order for the 11 to progress painlessly and become enlightened.

When 11 is a third pinnacle: Much travel, many aspects

of your work and love entanglements call on your time during this phase.

When 11 is a fourth pinnacle: It heralds the surprise factor, and there is no better number on which to spring surprise than the 11 vibration. Coming home to and teaching inner wisdom is the framework of this phase.

22

International acclaim, breaking through pain barriers to success

When 22 is a first pinnacle: The child may be off the starting block at a very young age. If so, he or she will be competitive, sport-oriented and acquisitive in the pocket-money or odd-job stakes.

When 22 is a second pinnacle: University and qualification take priority during the early second pinnacle. Career launching and finding their niche is imperative for 22s in their second pinnacle and into the middle years of the third.

When 22 is a third pinnacle: Being head-hunted is *de rigueur*. More likely, the carrier will be buying up companies.

When 22 is a fourth pinnacle: A high public profile is to your liking and you may become an authority on specialist subjects.

33

Healing, caring, witnessing truth

When 33 is a first pinnacle: Emotional guilt may be placed upon the young innocent. This is a taste of how the adult 33 might be able to help others in years to come.

When 33 is a second pinnacle: Your sense of responsibility will be high, so much so that you may be led through the nose to a fraught first marriage-type relationship.

When 33 is a third pinnacle: The committee factor will be high and the need for community recognition persistent. The family and their education will be your main priority.

When 33 is a fourth pinnacle: The 33 carrier may well be in a caring profession or associated with a humanitarian organisation. Contentment is the main feature of this phase.

INSIGHT NUMBERS

The insight number is the number which gives you an extra understanding of what you are doing, and why. It is most useful in the middle years, when you might be contemplating an affair (everybody who has been in a long-term relationship thinks about it sometimes . . . yes, they do!), changing professions, taking an Open University course or striking out on your own in a business venture, probably after the age of about thirty-six.

To find your insight year number, add together the digits of your life path number and your ability number and reduce. The combination of your life path and your ability number reminds you of your capabilities and your purpose and can be used throughout your life, but my feeling is that it is one to remember especially when you are laden with responsibility and need change but fear it a little, or a lot.

A 1 Insight Year: A year when you will more than likely be tempted to go it alone, to succeed, to claim the throne which is rightfully yours, to sell for profit or to make major change. It is an excellent year to open your own business and keep hold of the reins of power so that what success you breed does not turn into a monster.

A 2 Insight Year: A marvellous time to encourage and propagate anything in which you have a vested interest. The payoff in years to come will be good if you get it right now. A suitable time to start a family.

A 3 Insight Year: A year in which to lighten your load in some way and get in touch with fun again. A good time in which to graduate, find stimulus in the arts – writing or drama classes – for partying and showing others how versatile you are.

A 4 Insight Year: One of battening down the hatches and having a stock-check of all your assets. Keeping out of the reach of meddling individuals. It's a time to stick the raving on the back-burner and increase your productivity. Get your act together!

A 5 Insight Year: Encourages you to get the passport out of mothballs and it's up, up and away! 5 vibrates well with the planet earth and all her treasures. Intuition is high, and by trusting in the process of life you take another couple of steps up its marble staircase, two steps nearer the top.

A 6 Insight Year: Offers a heart-warming vibration of family and community relationships and refurbishment of the nest called home. During this time your profile in the world of committees and boards has the potential to be recognised and awarded.

A 7 Insight Year: Allows you to get in touch with the real you, your inner truth, through focusing your thoughts on what needs to be accomplished next in order for you to progress as you and not according to another's expectations of what you should be. When you follow your heart, you've got it made as a human being.

An 8 Insight Year: This is about picking the fruit you've grown over the years. A superb time to collect your dues and kick your heels in joy and celebration. Your abilities as a leader and compassionate friend are to the fore, with a bonus in financial matters more than a possibility because of the vibration of 8.

A 9 Insight Year: The year of winding down, of clearing up the debris of the past. Emotions should be handled carefully during this phase, and that would include dealing with relationships which are going nowhere so that you do not enter another nine-year life cycle burdened with all this junk. A year to be brave and bold in decision-making.

Part 3
What's in a name?

What's in a name? A plethora of information, plans, dreams, schemes – and potential. It is my belief that the intimate name, the Christian or first name, is the most important factor. Because of the custom of marriage and of a woman taking first her father's, then her husband's father's name, there is a tendency to become locked into the Second-hand Rose syndrome. No wonder the blushing bride becomes confused and often irritated in the first six months of marriage when others automatically change her name to Mrs Littlejohn when until the wedding she had been Ms Bigbob all her life. Related to this is the irritation we all feel when people call us by the wrong name. So what? So everything!

The persona is the part of our make-up, our psychology, which we use as a projector, a way of showing what we prefer the world to see. For example, a bank manager may lounge around at weekends in shorts, trainers and T-shirt, but he would never allow his investors to see him like that in business hours from Monday to Friday. A friend of mine cannot function without her 'lips' on. I personally prefer to face the world with my earrings *in situ*, and many office workers cannot speak to their boss or clients without a pen or pencil in their hand.

Numerology has an analytical practice for this and it is to be found in the letters contained within a name.

Names and numbers are like human beings. Just because you are a man or a woman it does not mean that is it. You are multi-dimensional, layered, full of secrets and intrigues.

When we meet or hear of someone with an embarrassing surname we laugh behind our hands or tease the unfortunate about it; give importance to it through a negative or positive response. The same applies to alphabetic number vibrations in that the positive and negative importance is contained within the name.

Name Changes

There are many reasons why people want to change their name. A name can cause pain through derision (we all know the jokes: 'To Mr and Mrs Pipe, a son Duane; to Jim and Betty Knutt, a daughter Hazel,' and so on). Some wish to dissociate themselves from a horrendous mother or father link. Writers, movie stars and people who desire high-profile lifestyles or professions often want to create a new image, or persona, in order to gain favour or recognition through making themselves appealing to others. There are just as many who have changed their names to avoid publicity in their private lives.

The urge to change a name may also, I believe, be rooted in the desire to bear the name one *chose* to come in with in the first place before, perhaps, the choice was blocked by domineering parents or guardians. In the same way our natural life paths and personalities are thwarted – sometimes temporarily, sometimes, sadly, for a lifetime – by significant others. We have to learn to relate to the numbers individually until we master the lesson of dealing with obstruction. I do not believe we can ditch the name or name vibration we chose to come into the world with. Now let me clarify that: the change people experience when success comes after a name change is not only material, but psychological, or logical in the psyche. The psyche – the real you – knows and feels comfortable when it proceeds as intended.

I also subscribe to my own theory that people who carry two names are working out two lives concurrently. If 'stars' took time to understand that they were living on double rations and lived accordingly we would have fewer 'I survived birds/boys, booze 'n' drugs' tales of woe. The implications of juggling two lives in one skin are huge but possible. What's in a name? A persona, a psyche and an ability vibration. The old chestnut actual or would-be stars trot out holds a lot of truth. At cocktail parties they talk about themselves (yet again): 'I was on Rodeo Drive the other day and this guy comes up to me and says, "Hey, didn't you used to be . . .", and I said, "I still am!" '

Before you change your name, then, consider carefully why you want to make such an important decision. My own opinion is that there is no need to do so: it does not enhance the vibration because every number has a positive, ideal and negative vibration. You can't just ditch a learning curve. If you do rejoice in a name like Horace Lavatoryworth and decide to change it, then it is imperative that you take on board the lessons of the original name.

The same applies to a married name or to whether or not you use a middle name, or shortened name, a nickname and so on. Allow the second lessons, the name-change lessons, to be valid but of lesser importance in the overall picture of the real you.

The name vibration is segmented into three major parts:
the persona, the psyche and the ability values. The
persona number is derived from the numerical value of
the consonants in our name, the psyche number from the
numerical value of the vowels and the ability number
from the full numerical value of the whole name. Each
letter of the alphabet has a numerical value, shown
below, which is used to calculate each part:

A	B	C	D	E	F	G	H	I
1	2	3	4	5	6	7	8	9

J	K	L	M	N	O	P	Q	R
1	2	3	4	5	6	7	8	9

S	T	U	V	W	X	Y	Z
1	2	3	4	5	6	7	8

THE PERSONA NUMBER

The persona number is derived from the consonants in
your name. The persona is how we prefer the world to
see us – our projection, darlings! It allows others to get a
calculated insight into us. For instance, if I wanted you
to believe I belong to an élite Sloane set, I would wear,
as an archetypal example, the obligatory black velvet
Alice band, a green or navy waxed jacket, a string of
pearls and carry my Filofax. If I were a bank manager I

would wear a business suit to indicate that I mean business. How many Hawaiian shirts and shorts have you seen at the Stock Exchange in London or New York, two bastions of the persona? Unfortunately too often uniform statements are a sham, the stress foundation where we major in psychosomatic distress: the conman posing as a lord, the robber in a policeman's uniform. When running at average the persona is a fairly truthful attempt at letting others know how you feel and what you think. This cuts both ways: when we think we know someone or might get to like them more, we suddenly notice their scruffy down-at-heel shoes. Something tells us that this person might be slapdash, or at best has got dressed in the dark!

To calculate the persona number add together the value of the consonants in the name being analysed, using the table on p.104.

The name on the first example birth certificate is Suzy Jane Pink. To find out how she prefers the world to see her, we have to select the consonants in her name:

S	U	Z	Y		J	A	N	E		P	I	N	K
1		8	7		1		5			7		5	2

Now add all the consonants together and reduce them to a single digit or master number where applicable: $1 + 8 + 7 + 1 + 5 + 7 + 5 + 2 = 36$; $3 + 6 = 9$.

The Meaning of the Persona Numbers

1

You wish to use power and to be seen to use power. A self-publicist, you are always on the front page, whether in reality or metaphorically. Head boy or girl, team leader, group organiser, first in line at Harrods sale. You can be a tyrant if you refuse to understand fully the wise use of power.

Motto: I was here first

2

Should anyone rumble your darker side you will white-wash Vesuvius to convince him of your loyalty and kindness. You can be guilty of wearing your heart on your sleeve, but on the whole you are a good egg. You can be lazy if not motivated or being employed to the full.

Motto: Have a cup of tea, luvvie

3

Strike up the band, number 3 is here! Fanfares, feather boas . . . and the women are even more extravagant. 3s are like New York, they love a parade. The worst thing you could tell a 3 is that you feel sorry for him and offer help. They do all the helping, thank you very much, and can be sarcastic if riled, critical if unprogressed.

Motto: Peel me a grape before my bungee jump, darling

4

The office is going out to party but the serious 4 has work to do. She's either catching up or expanding an idea. Don't you know there's a war on? is the 4's watchword. Seriously, though, a very reliable if somewhat sensible persona, often fastidious. 4s are often good at handing out reproachful looks if you leave on time. A negative 4 can be chaotic, slapdash or apathetic.

Motto: Life is a deal

5

A poem, a chocolate, a romantic gesture or a beautifully wrapped gift is the 5's way of communicating. Watch them giggle, wriggle and exit if they feel hemmed in. Soft and dreamy is the 5 look. A negative 5 is unrealistic and a dreamer.

Motto: When's the next plane to . . .?

6

The first words the 6 probably said were committee, home and art gallery. The innovative 6 needs a broad canvas to paint on and, never a worker bee, the recognition to go with it. They need and supply information – and yes, that means they gossip too. Watch what you tell them – a negative 6 can be a witch.

Motto: I volunteer to be president

7

He's the one who is still reading as the library blazes: he's just found a piece on pyromania and finds it fascinating. The 7 strolls between distant or extremely informative. Knowledge is power to 7s, and they are ace teachers when motivated, pedantic if unprogressed.

Motto: Shhh, I'm thinking

8

Family values exude from the 8 and others may feel inferior as the unwitting 8 coos and clucks around her grateful brood. The 8 is a great persona due to the many storms he or she has had to weather. Trust me, I'm an 8, is their watchword. They can be dismissive if unfulfilled.

Motto: You're not going to Buckingham Palace without a good breakfast in you

9

Lord and Lady Bountiful gestures are the indicators of the 9. Generous to a fault, they can be overwhelming if over-exercising their persona or ignored. They will also be found coordinating facts and putting people in touch with each other. They are not clever with money and often come a cropper through excessive luxury spending.
Motto: Don't put the caviare dish on my overdraft statement

10

The 10 is the person you admire for getting there against the odds. He wins the marathon with a broken leg and a migraine, she has her first baby at forty-one after adopting two orphans ten years ago. The 10 knows all about heaven and earth and the struggle needed to cope with both at times. They are in constant turmoil if they give up trying.
Motto: Mountains are for climbing

11

The 11s are smiling benefactors with a penchant for giving accurate psychic information about an event, or for giving the other side of a debate with insight. Enlightenment is their medium. Don't waste their time or you'll never see them again. Negative 11s are petty, prone to lying and dreamers.
Motto: I think therefore I can

22

Bow your head, here comes the successful tycoon. On second thoughts, don't – watch how she does it. The 22 persona has great presence and an eye for a takeover bid. The subject of that takeover could be your husband or wife. You may recognise a negative 22 by their ruthlessness.

Motto: Can it turn a dollar?

33

Walking through the war zone, mopping brows and soothing fears, the healing 33 persona is the rainbow after the storm. They will stand by you when all others have scampered. A negative one will whinge for the Olympic team, often favouring depression to action.

Motto: I'm here

Suzy Jane Pink's persona number is 9, suggesting she prefers the world to recognise her 'superb' information skills – at 15 per cent, thank you. She's also perfected the dubious knack of presenting other people's ideas as her own. Financial denial is not something she recognises; the overdraft was made for her.

THE PSYCHE NUMBER

The vowels within a name, whether a person's name or a company name, show the potential for the very personal self, the inner truth of the psyche. This is the part which is the reckoner, the real you as you curl up in the duvet just before sleep, the part of you that knows what really happened in a situation. The psyche is the big knowing. But do we use it well? Very few do.

Carl Jung would call this the racial memory, the part which knows what to do and how to do it but is not exercised enough by some. Oh, how I wish we would use it more often – it would cast asunder the obstacles we put in our own paths. For instance: you earn £2,000 a month.

You have a friend you admire or envy who has a house in a prestigious area that you would love to live in, but you would need £2,500 a month to realistically afford it. You also like going abroad on holiday once a year, buying lots of nice clothes and going to the movies, theatre and dining out. But the house you *must* have, and you push and squeeze and you check the biscuit tin to get the extra credit rating to raise a mortgage on a house like that. Your psyche knows that you cannot afford that sort of commitment without enormous sacrifice. Does it stop you? Is the Pope a Catholic . . .

The outcome, unless you are extremely fortunate with a windfall or hike in pay, is that two years down the line you are living to work, to pay for the brick necklace you have chosen for yourself. You conveniently don't remember that you did it to yourself, you blame it on the recession and succumb to stress. What's that got to do with the psyche? Everything. In your truth box, your psyche, you know that all you needed was a roof over your head, and time to learn the lessons you have to learn. In effect what you have done is blocked your exciting path with destructive binding ritual and social peer pressure. Take a look into the eyes of Mother Teresa, the Dalai Lama, the child who has found an unusually coloured pebble on the beach, and see all you really need. It is not wrong to be ambitious or aspire but it is criminal to block your life path with self-burdening.

By welcoming the psyche, our inner truth, and its rightful healthy platform in our lives, we elevate and free ourselves for a more comfortable and simpler but richer level of existence. It does not necessarily make life Easy Street, but a clear perspective is a wonderful window to

110

view from. It is created on the inside and affects how we see the outside.

The psyche number lets us know more about the core self, the true self. The psyche is the centre of power and wisdom within all of us which knows what to do and how to do it. It is rarely shown. An example would be the mother whose child is under threat. She often flies at the attacker like a banshee and with a ferocious strength she could never consciously muster. Another example might be your feelings in a conversation with someone who is constantly criticising you. You are desperate to run or tell the bore to shut up, but social training, which can lead to fear of confrontation, restricts you. Instead you are polite, saying nothing or pretending to be sorry that the other person feels that way. This is the psyche being blocked unnaturally, because in the wee small hours you can be wide awake, still seething at being so abused. The psyche is an invaluable insight into what we truly feel.

So back to Suzy Jane Pink. Next we want to find out what her psyche number is. To do this we select the vowels from her name, using the numerical values laid out on p.104. The values of the vowels are:

$$\begin{array}{ccccc} A & E & I & O & U \\ 1 & 5 & 9 & 6 & 3 \end{array}$$

$$\begin{array}{ccc} \text{S U Z Y} & \text{J A N E} & \text{P I N K} \\ 3 & 1 \quad 5 & 9 \end{array}$$

$3 + 1 + 5 + 9 = 18; 1 + 8 = 9.$

Suzy Jane Pink's psyche number is 9. This lets us know that her true self, her secret self is a lover of peace and harmony with a penchant for the finer things in life. She won't skimp on quality and is good at sharing with others. If living negatively she has the potential to be superficial and a taker.

Now you know how to calculate a name vibration, dip into the meanings shown next, either with the examples given, or with the names of friends or colleagues or your own name analysis.

The simple and straightforward way to lay out any name for analysis is by numbering the vowels above the name and the consonants below, as shown in the following.

Vowels	5 6	5	5	1	1
	GEORGE	BERNARD		SHAW	
Consonants	7 9 7	2 9 5 9 4		2 8 5	

Vowels = 23; 2 + 3 = 5
Consonants = 67; 6 + 7 = 13; 1 + 3 = 4

The Meaning of the Psyche Numbers

1

You are a person who needs a logical pattern to all things. You battle away in the background for position and power until you are sure you can show your hand. You are the office boy who dreams of being a director of the company and goes on to realise that dream. The MENSA test is your idea of relaxation because it is both enjoyable and rates you at the end. You must be free to be yourself at all costs. You do not take kindly to anyone giving you orders, and command respect at all levels. One thing you may fail to understand is the dependency of weaker people on you. You want to be boss, yet anger easily when others allow you to take them over. You have to learn to be a leader of quality as opposed to a leader in name only. You will need to develop the art of listening to the opinions of others as well as being listened to before making a correct decision. The 1 is encouraged to remember that others are not lesser mortals but on different learning curves. Your natural ability to lead and govern is magnificent, but only when your heart is in the job.

Advice: Listen and talk

Avoid: Dictating

When operating negatively: Bully, tyrant and zealous critic can fit the 1

Parents of a 1 child: The 1 as a child will need much stimulation, and his progress at school should be supervised closely from home in order to give him a flying start in academia. *Suggested gifts*: Anything connected with coordination skills, including dance lessons, book tokens, theatre trips, Scalextrix.

2

The most powerful weapon in peace is a table to sit around and find a solution, and United Nations negotiations would hold no fears for you. 2s won't shout, but they will serve tea and sympathy to encourage a successful outcome. You would make an excellent philosopher or Soroptomist. Make talk not war; anything for a quiet life. 2s are the pacifists of numerology, but tend to be worriers. Try to realise that to understand 'give' you must also understand 'take', and you can't have one without the other. 2s often have good ideas but hold back just a little too long only for someone else to pinch the limelight. You must learn that it can be a beautiful day out there if only you pop your head out of the door. You hold back unnecessarily and must take heart in confrontational situations. 2s love to work out everything in their heads before making a move. Their ability to soothe fevered brows is legendary.

Advice: Be optimistic

Avoid: Being manipulated

When operating negatively: Depressive, victimised, whingers

Parents of a 2 child: Don't push the child beyond its immediate capability. The 2 is sensitive and the world of music or service may appeal later in life. Parents are advised to remember that we are not all cut out to be brain surgeons or performing seals. Nurture the child's self-esteem especially in the early stages and in early teenage years. A 2 who experienced a traumatic birth needs gentle handling emotionally. *Suggested gifts*: Pretty things with sensitive colours, dolls, garages, anything to do with human caring or service.

3

Performing centre-stage at Covent Garden Opera House is just a fragment of what passes through the fantasy mind of the 3. Yellow rubber gloves become the jewel-encrusted gauntlets of a prince as the washing-up bowl transforms into the frothy dangerous ocean beneath the coastal fortress walls. Meanwhile, back on earth, the gas bill has gone past the red reminder stage and all hell breaks loose. The delightfully dippy 3 is the carer in numerology, but at worse he or she can be a martyr. In the pursuit of making others comfortable in order to gain favour, they often forget to acknowledge life's number one lesson: take care of yourself fully before trying to give to gain approval. 3s are very good at sharing and can be hurt when others do not reciprocate. Optimistic and nurturing to a fault, they make excellent stage mothers, ferrying their brood between one dance class and another. They must guard against becoming martyrs to a caring cause as they have a tendency to pour out a gallon of love in order to receive a drop. 3s love to be heard and must have a platform to sound off from.

Advice: Allow your sense of humour to carry you

Avoid: Carelessness in business and personal relationships

When operating negatively: Tactless, erratic, negligent

Parents of a 3 child: Learn to live with young Hector or Primrose trying to fly from the garage roof. This kid is spontaneous beyond your wildest nightmares. However, he or she is lovable, daring and innovative and may benefit from some friendly advice from a favourite aunt or uncle when you are biting the carpet in frustration. *Suggested gifts*: Manacles, straitjacket . . . seriously, though, any action toy, computer technology, chess set, chemistry set (but only under your supervision!).

4

The 4 was probably born at work or was wrapped up in an accountancy spreadsheet before being weighed. You feel safer in the sensible world of order and pattern, but if you are operating negatively it's five steps forward and eight back in the tango of chaos. You must avoid martyrdom and oppressive organisations or tyrant bosses. The Filofax was invented for the 4. Practical, neat, organised – and you can remove evidence quickly! Tidiness in act and thought is imperative for the 4 to survive. You can be a workaholic, or on a negative level bore everyone into kingdom come with what you are going to do, but never do it. The 4 can become so absorbed in work that it is a perfect breeding ground for stress. All in all, 4s are admired for high standards. Organised, reliable and diligent, you must be careful not to let success go to your head. Remember to have fun: you can always turn up at a barbecue in a suit and tie just in case you have to go back to work. The negative 4 is never satisfied and never reaches deadlines without a panic. They have the ability, but do not use their extraordinary energy levels to their advantage.

Advice: Loosen up but never slacken

Avoid: Pessimism

When operating negatively: Manipulative, wolf in sheep's clothing, clingy

Parents of a 4 child: Learn to live with the child's quirky and sometimes ritualistic ways. You may also have to adhere to the child's fastidiousness, such is the orderliness of the 4 child's mind. He will argue and negotiate until the cows come home, so practise a few escape routes such as 'bed now, junior!' Remember who is boss. *Suggested gifts*: Calligraphy set, brass-rubbing kit, 1,000 mathematical problems, squash racquet.

5

I wandered lonely as a 5 that floats on high o'er vales and . . . the romantic 5 must have peace, joy and harmony in order to survive the harshness of life's reality. But the 5 is not weak, and loves to travel. You are happy in the Kasbah, Macchu Picchu, or Brent Cross Shopping Centre, but never in the kitchen with a mop. 5 does not do Cinderella work, and that's final. Self-employment is the answer, with a Buttons to motivate you. Boredom is a prison cell for the sociable, freedom-loving 5. A Saturday night in watching TV is second only to death. You are not always a nightclubber – 5s love hill-walking and being by the sea, as long as there is something to see or do. Hang-gliding in the Himalayas and canoeing around Cape Horn are the stimuli needed to satiate your taste for adventure. Clip the 5's wings and he or she will stagnate mentally – restriction is not a welcome word in his vocabulary. If the 5 had his way every day would be a party. As a 5 you must concentrate your energies on feathering a nest for your later years, as well as being the life and soul of the party now. 5s often reach maturity feeling unfocused and disoriented if they don't get their act together around their mid-twenties. The 5 needs poetry, romance and music to survive the everyday things in life and must be bombarded with radio, TV and newspapers to keep in close touch. The outcome of such a lifestyle is that they seek tranquillity and solace in their middle years and may be found in their country cottage or by the sea taking much welcome breaks. 5s are extremists.

Advice: Travel to learn instead of brag

Avoid: The multi-marriage path will cost you dearly

When operating negatively: Can be disruptive, quick-mouthed, flirtatious

Parents of a 5 child: Lock the front gate as soon as she takes her first steps, for that's where she's heading. The 5 child will be glued to television wildlife or geography programmes and may well be able to quote the gross national product of every country. The 5 is a lover of the beautiful aspects of life and can be very – sometimes too – trusting. *Suggested gifts*: Travel books/videos, visiting the flight deck of your holiday jet, exchange student programmes, poetry books, watercolours.

6

Prudish you may be called by others, but positive and responsible you are to you. Never give up your standards in favour of the unstable fast finishes. You were born with a clipboard under your arm and hand raised to eyebrow, facing the horizon of position and authority. Encourage a 6 child's creative streak and allow him to be your DIY helper – he will use it to the hilt later in life. The 6s are the engineers of numerology, always curious about why something is working. Information is power to them. They are so curious that they are not averse to looking through the private papers of others, not out of malice, just to have more information. A positive 6 is one of the most hospitable of hosts. His home is a shrine to good taste and creativity. He may even deal in antiques and fine art to indulge and profit from her need to be surrounded by all things bright and beautiful. 6s need to create a perfect environment and can interfere with the natural pace of those around them. The negative 6 must learn not to take out his shortcomings on his offspring. If a positive 6 is creative then a negative 6 is surely destructive.

Advice: Create with love, not for a price

Avoid: Social power struggles

When operating negatively: Snobbish, power-seeking, destructive

Parents of a 6 child: You must not fall for the 6 child's attempts to pacify with a gift or trade-off. Behaviour such as this will build a monster in adulthood who responds only to snobbery, and equates success with deals and backhanders. The 6 child would also benefit from understanding that the home is a haven and not just a wardrobe. *Suggested gifts*: Monopoly, Scrabble, a dolls' house; anything with a perforated edge, a rubber stamp – they like playing offices.

7

The Scarlet Pimpernel of numerology, the elusive 7 is always off doing special work but mostly analysing why: why something isn't working and why it is working. Religion or religious service often attracts the 7. Never, but never, interrupt a 7 as he is probably solving the meaning of life, so engrossed is he in things of the higher mind. They can eccentrically forget they actually live on the planet. Like 11s they are sensitive to noise, preferring the peace and tranquillity of the attic, countryside or library. The 7 must remember to go to the shops, take a holiday and feed the cat. He can become so engrossed in his own world of contemplation that he sometimes forgets the basic functions of communicating through socialising. As a marriage partner a 7 is reliable and prefers fireside reading and the pensive life to one of garish pleasure. 7s are spiritual beings who know a lot and feel a lot. They must take care not to succumb to maudlin thoughts and loss of purpose.

Advice: Read and seed

Avoid: Bickering and time-wasters

When operating negatively: Withdrawn, elusive, penny-pinching

Parents of a 7 child: You will be aware from an early stage that your child prefers to live in his head. You will also have to learn that the 7 child demands privacy and, except in extreme circumstances, never transgress their secret files or hiding places. The 7 loves knowledge and in that secret place may be nothing more sinister than a picture which intrigues his curious mind. So spiritual is the 7 child that the parent may learn a lot from his imaginary friends and from investigating the background to such 'friends'. *Suggested gifts*: Bible, Koran, Torah; general knowledge books; any construction toy, pottery or sculpting tools.

8

Visualise the 8 as the hub of a wheel. Nothing much happens for a wheel without a hub, but once they are together they can travel great distances. This is why 8s often make great travellers or investigative journalists. They are always near adventure and at the centre of things with a truthful account of what has just happened. They know a lot about synchronicity through experience. There are many ways of gaining experience, and the 8 usually learns the hard way, often finding herself an innocent pawn in someone else's game. It must be said that this is not a lifetime element; once the lesson is learned and experience gained, the 8 can attain high office in many walks of life. Emotion is a feeling which is high on the 8's priorities.

Advice: Strive. You'll make it. Flow

Avoid: Narrow-mindedness and stubbornness

When operating negatively: Accident-prone, tense, distant

Parents of an 8 child: You are blessed with an honest child with a most loving nature. However, be prepared to batten down the hatches and take part in a few stand-offs in determination – yours versus hers. The odd thing with the 8 child is that even though she might feel confident at home she can be bullied at school. An 8 child's sensitivity must be handled with care, so watch for the moodiness and depression that could affect her and nip it in the bud. 8s are said to be difficult to live with, but they are great witnesses of life. They are observant and may attain great business or home acumen after hard work during their lifetime. They keep their heads down to ride out the storms they have to weather at points in their life. To cancel out the theory that 0 does not exist, take a close look at the two circles which make up an 8. The top circle is the spiritual world and the bottom the material world. The 8 has to learn to strike a comfortable balance between matters of the higher mind and the work which has to be completed on the planet this time round. *Suggested gifts*: Model-making kits; pets; friends over to stay regularly (this is advantageous to the strengthening of the 8 child's self-esteem).

9

You are on the wrong side of gullible and must take great care who you associate with. Be aware of clingers who would love to take full advantage of your status and luxury-loving lifestyle. You can have a problem with the duality of the 9: shall I, shan't I? were probably the first words you spoke. Attention-loving 9s must understand that the spiritual side must be attended to during this lifetime, and the pleasures of the flesh and mind-altering substances or liquids do you no favours. On the surface the 9 is egotistical, competent and vain. Dig deeper and you will find underneath a kind, loving, slipper-clad pussycat. They love the latest fashions and dandyish gestures if male. They possess good intuitive powers but are prone to exaggeration. They are catalysts for information and so do not keep secrets or confidences well. They must constantly remind themselves to walk in the light. The 9 wants to experience life to the full and can do so if she knows how to curb her excesses. The nature of the 9 is naturally loving – and often! 9s need a lot of space and make dubious marriage partners, and a nine-to-five job is a prison sentence for them.

Advice: Dare, care and share

Avoid: Selfishness, paranoia and perpetual personal conflict

When operating negatively: Egotistical, dismissive, time-consuming

Parents of a 9 child: Keep a tin of biscuits and a spare duvet for the waifs and strays the 9 child thinks need a home like his or hers. She is popular and generally enjoys that status for the rest of her life. There is, however, a tendency for the 9 child to exaggerate and be ridiculed, which is the negative side of the 9 vibration. Generous to a fault, she can be manipulated by the occasional cunning child who sneaks into her crowd of friends. *Suggested gifts*: World Wide Fund for Nature subscription; reinforced pockets (their pocket money burns straight through!); geology hammer for fossil-searching on the beach; drama classes.

10

Just when you think you are getting somewhere some circumstance no one could have foreseen thwarts your progress. This is the lot of the 10 at several major junctures in his or her life. I have a theory that the 10 has been a 1 who has misused power in a previous life, for the 10, like the 1, has the potential for enormous success, but only after a struggle or following a hurdle-strewn path. You must learn to lead without persecution and to realise your spiritual progression without restricting others. To say that the 10 is the conqueror of numerology would be no understatement, and once she has realised that there is no such thing as a free lunch she is on her way to freedom, the constructive use of power and contentment. 10s may often find that in the social playground they are either liked or disliked – there is no middle ground with a 10.

Advice: Reassess your progress and do not be led. You know you won't like the consequences, you trainee 1, you!

Avoid: False flattery for your skills

When operating negatively: Morose, woeful, unmotivated

Parents of a 10 child: Don't panic – he'll get there in the end like the rest of us, just a bit later, and as a result he'll be a lot wiser than most. You will need to support the child and then let him symbolically fall now and again to gather self-confidence. There can be learning difficulties with this vibration, and patience pays off. The 10 must remain true to truth and learn the difference between the real world and Walter Mitty's. *Suggested gifts*: Discipline, and the teaching of respect for others without being servile. He may be your baby but he has a lesson to learn like the rest of us. A pet to care for, any logistics game, any integrative board game. It is important for the 10 child to learn that it's safe to lose now and again without throwing a tantrum.

11

Life lifts you up where you belong, or it should. You have one foot on the planet and one foot off. As a master number you will be more sensitive to slights and cruel words than most. Noise is also a problem for you as your hearing is more highly tuned than that of lesser mortals. The intuition of the 11 is second to none due to journeys off-planet, and any 11 denying his or her life path or psyche number can feel very disgruntled. 11s often choose to walk alone in life. Their healing and psychic abilities make them the batteries to which everyone else attaches their leads for energy and inspiration. The 11 has a mission to teach and illuminate the darker side of those in trouble. The lovely 11 is a joy to be around. You see behind a false exterior and nurture the positive elements hidden beneath the lie. 11s are always in the service of others and ask little in return. Things come their way as they often know that universal law provides everything unconditionally.

Advice: Shine your light where there is darkness

Avoid: Petty crime, shady partnerships and strife

When operating negatively: They can become egotistical and vain, gaining no credit, only antagonism for the brash display of their power. Critical, duplicitous, but often come off worst themselves

Parents of an 11 child: Are you sitting down? Your child is on a mission: you'd better get used to it and be aware that you are working for the kid. Don't panic – I was only half serious. The 11 child's intuition when operating in a nurturing environment is a wonderful learning curve for the observer as well as the child. He will be gentle, informed and expressive about the basics and good things in human beings and the planet. Never stand on a fly in the presence of an 11 child – he will fret for days. They are less likely than other numbers to become millionaires, but have the potential to be billionaires in human understanding and inner beauty. *Suggested gifts*: Spiritual understanding; origami kits; a gift of a painting or print; tools and materials to make things for a humanitarian cause.

22

You want to build a suspension bridge, spacecraft or underwater city? Ask a 22. And then, in the afternoon . . . The master number 22 is here to utilise power in the most positive and humane way. The trouble is that when a master number is crooked it is not a pretty experience for associates. When a 22 is crooked, book a flight to anywhere, or suffer. Once the 22 reaches the top of the mountain the view is breathtaking, but the climb can be perilous and heavy going if he or she tries to deviate from truth, wisdom and human respect. Do not become daunted by the enormity of your abilities, but go forward in a steady climb to reach your peak. Once you believe in you, nothing can halt your rise to greatness. Many things of the higher mind may be revealed to you during your lifetime. Many 22s experience great inner conflict because of the vast library of knowledge they carry. They often attain high profile in the commercial world. When the master number 22 operates on a negative level it can be one of the nastiest energies. Many criminals are negative 22s and use their abilities to undermine others.

Advice: Go for it in the most positive and energetic manner

Avoid: Duplicity and money-laundering

When operating negatively: Because of their enormous power negative 22s can be despotic. They are easily drawn into underground movements, robbery and violence.

Parents of a 22 child: Refuse pocket money and he'll come up with an award-winning scheme to finance himself. We are talking trainee presidents of international companies here, and, make no mistake, you have a potential magnate on your fireside rug. Beautiful he may be – smarmily cute he is not. 22s are so practical that they only hug at Christmas and birthdays. (Well, it's the WIFM factor, isn't it? – what's in it for me?) He'll be the highest-paid paper person on his run with a bulging piggy bank on the windowsill to bear testimony to it. I hear you saying, 'You're not having a motorbike!' and him 'I've got enough in my building society to buy one, anyway.' The 22 child often prefers solitude on the way to the top and plays his cards close to his chest. He will buy you a mansion from the spoils, but don't expect to see him every week. *Suggested gifts*: One share in a company; chemistry set (but not with a 3 playmate, please, we're talking nuclear fission here!); a gold or oil divining rod; any board game which collects currency as proof of winning. Poker is not recommended, Dad, unless you are trying to avoid capital transfer tax for fun!

33

The darling 33 is available twenty-four hours a day and must learn to take care of him or herself in order to survive excessive and depleting worrying in the vibration he has chosen. The 33 painter or writer will work all through the night for six weeks and still produce Nobel Prize quality. A banner carrier, the 33 will be well known as a person who gets things done, often without thanks. They carry the traits of the 6: 3 + 3 =

6, and are motivators, facilitators and great organisers. 33s offer the world a shoulder to cry on and sometimes they feel as if the weight of the world is on their shoulders. Because of their intuition they feel others' pain more easily and must protect themselves against people who drain their energies. Many people may come to a 33 for help and a more able person would be hard to find. The medical or healing professions, whether complementary or orthodox, may draw you and your ability to see beyond a symptom will be acute. Your gift is to create peace where there is strife, beauty where there is barrenness, but you must guard against being used by organisations to fire the metaphoric bullets for their cause. If a carrier of 33 finds this master number too hard to carry, reduce it to a 6 and languish in the hospitable, design-oriented vibration of the 6.

Advice: Heal and grow from your experiences as a 33

Avoid: Martyrdom

When operating negatively: Obstructive, cruel, victimised, martyr

Parents of a 33 child: The birds and bees and the sycamore trees are friends of the 33 child. She is on a very special journey and it is often a privilege to parent such a number. The gentle, pensive 33 child may cause the parent some angst simply because she feels so much, and so deeply. Well, the good news is that the 33 vibration is probably more evolved than you and she is just taking life at her pace. Allow the child to enjoy the childhood years for the adult life will be paved with variation: some brilliance, but nevertheless tough. *Suggested gifts*: Nurse's outfit (in fact any emergency service outfit); the United National

Charter for bedtime reading; two orphans to look after; 'saint' inscribed on her bedroom door; my telephone number . . .

THE ABILITY NUMBER

The ability number is derived from the numerical value of the vowels and consonants of your full name at birth. It reveals the skills you chose to study and succeed in before you came in this time by offering opportunity and insight into career options and capabilities. It is your task number; your promise to yourself to learn a certain lesson. Do note the words *chosen to succeed in before you came in*. Pause for a moment and ask yourself if you have honestly kept your word to yourself, or have you been waylaid by trying to reduce yourself to suit the rules of others?

The ability number can be changed, often to enhance a life path. Many actors, writers and musicians change their names, to enhance not only the sound of their name but also the numerical vibration of it alongside their life path. This said, I refer you to my earlier theory that if you change your name you are running two life paths instead of one. Analyse both, especially at the pinnacles (see pp.86–97). It is important to note, though, that a pure and full numerology chart will always have the date of birth, the original name on the birth certificate, and the name the person is known by. This is supported by the theory that not only do we choose our parents when we are between lives, but it is we who choose the name we carry. The numbers have several layers of truth, and later in this book we deal with three meanings per number. Again, a good tip is not to try to memorise everything, simply remember the opposite of the initial positive meaning when applicable.

The ability number stengthens and helps to realise the potential of the life path. As we have seen with the persona number and psyche number, each letter of the alphabet has a numerical vibration and meaning:

A	B	C	D	E	F	G	H	I
1	2	3	4	5	6	7	8	9
J	K	L	M	N	O	P	Q	R
1	2	3	4	5	6	7	8	9
S	T	U	V	W	X	Y	Z	
1	2	3	4	5	6	7	8	

Now we wish to know Suzy Jane Pink's ability number. This is calculated by adding together the persona number and the psyche number.

Persona Number: 9
Psyche Number: 9
$9 + 9 = 18; 1 + 8 =$ 9

Therefore, Suzy's ability number is 9, showing us that if she is operating positively she is aware of world situations and her compassionate nature has the potential to allow her to put people in touch with each other on a global scale. As a 9 she is a coordinator of people and situations. If operating negatively she is bigoted and self-seeking.

We can use the grid again here to file the numerical vibration for assessment, e.g.:

```
L I N D A    L O U I S E    M A R C H E
3 9 5 4 2    3 6 3 9 1 5    4 1 9 3 8 5  = 80
```

Noting 0 as a completed cycle and ancient skill, she has come through into this lifetime with and adding that note to the vibration of 8 she carries:

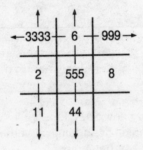

Linda Louise Marche is an ability number 8, indicating that she may prefer a more exciting, but organised career or lifestyle. Her grid indicates, through her completed trait lines of organisation, logic and independence, that she is a person who can get things done for herself and others. She's extremely logical and trusts herself. Remember to refer to the multiple

130

numbers in a chart analysis when doing a name or date of birth.

The Meaning of the Ability Numbers

1

The ability to be Mr/Ms Big in the world of commerce. You are not too good at taking orders and prefer to associate with the leaders of a company rather than the minions. You must guard against a destructive critical streak when operating negatively.

Suggested profession: Manager, politician, priest, shipper

2

A backroom worker who is reliable and a good partner to have. The 2s' capacity for kindness and understanding is strong, with the added bonus of diplomacy in their favour. When operating negatively they can become a dogsbody and over-sensitivity can be a major block.

Suggested profession: Carer, personal assistant, craft worker, healer, therapist

3

The optimistic 3 bounds with energy but must take into consideration the personality of others before bombarding them with the 'wow' factor. The world is his oyster providing he remembers to rest like other mere mortals. The worst aspects of the 3 are shallowness, exaggeration and masking true feelings with gushiness.

Suggested profession: Nurse, marriage guidance counsellor, actor, explorer

4

The logistics expert of the numbers. As a 4 be prepared to work long hours, and if you enjoy your work you won't mind at all. Do, however, remember that your family and loved ones might like to see you too, and do not expect your staff to be as in love with work as you are. 4s need to keep tabs on their stubborn streak, which can lead to financial ruin through a blinkered outlook.

Suggested profession: Architect, engineer, chef, tailor

5

The adventurer/explorer of the numbers with a capacity for reaching the giddy heights of fame through his or her love of life. The 5 needs stimulus and can be claustrophobic in nature. As children 5s become bored easily and must avoid turning to illegal or mind-altering substances just because they are having to sit still for five minutes.

Suggested profession: Actor, poet, gigolo, DJ, publican, scriptwriter

6

The great mediator, the 6 has the capacity to be the core of the office or community through his or her understanding of fundamental issues. She manages to juggle family life and business life to everyone's advantage. The home is most important to 6s, with their creative eye noticeable. As teenagers they will be fashion-conscious leaders.

Suggested profession: Teacher, doctor, nurse, community coordinator

7

Find the book then look behind it for the 7. A sponge for facts, figures and phenomena, the 7 is a philosophical and spiritual teacher who will be much admired by his or her students. Never expect too much from the 7, because he is often aware that he is on a mission and any partner would do well to take note of this very early on in the relationship. 7s do have to remember that they have earth work to do too, and must let their hair down now and again.

Suggested profession: Astronaut, monk, philosopher, lighthouse-keeper, lecturer

8

The 8s are here to learn about striking balance in their abilities, and once they have mastered that they are on the road to a most fulfilling lifetime. The 8 is a high achiever, both in business and in family matters. When operating negatively they do have the potential to go over the top with ambition, which can lead to burn-out.

Suggested profession: Broker, underwriter, round-the-world yachtsman, investigative journalist

9

The 9 is here to bring people, information and situations together. A witness to the power of synchronicity, a 9 needs to be needed and is well suited to a high-profile position in commerce or industry, with a spotlight on the communication industries such as radio, television and the written word. When operating negatively they can be accused of plagiarism, developing an inflated persona or being negatively self-oriented.

Suggested profession: Broadcaster, gambler, wit, bon viveur, model, recluse

10

Generally has a PhD in the word 'struggle'. You must be
encouraged to keep on a level path of thought and
actions. Your tenacity is much admired, and just when
everyone thought it was all over for poor 10, up she
comes with an astonishing idea or burst of energy. The
potential winner in the 10 will only sink if she wallows in
self-pity and becomes resentful. You must always
remember that you have the same energy as the 1 but a
few more obstacles to overcome. When 10s get their act
together and understand that the world is not against
them they develop into a kinder type of 1.
Suggested profession: Architect, builder, police chief,
vet

11

The lonely path of the 11 is often mistaken for avoidance
of intimacy, but when operating positively the 11 knows
where he is going and savours the many experiences,
both physical and spiritual, along the way. 11 is here to
shine light where there is fear of darkness and to lighten
unnecessary burdens. When operating negatively the 11
can be overpowering and can misread the wants and
needs of others who are not ready to be shown the way.
This would apply to the 11 healer who tells people what
is wrong with them without being invited to comment.
Suggested profession: Healer, iridologist, psychic, overseas voluntary worker

22

The 22 has the enviable appearance of being able to walk
on thin air, such is the confidence she exudes. Monaco,
marinas and casinos are the natural environment of

materially successful 22s as learning to use and enjoy power is part of the lesson they have to learn. But this superficial lifestyle is unfulfilling as a learning curve unless your corporation is working for the welfare of humanity and not just an acquisitive self. When operating negatively the 22 ability is one of deception and fraudulent or criminal activity with the emphasis on corruption at government or military level.

Suggested professions: Magician, director of huge corporation, comedian, scientist

33

Saint or depressive. Sorry, but there is no middle ground with the 33. One of the most humanitarian numbers, 33 is the healer, soother and calmer of woes. Your energy level when operating positively is extremely high and you are a master of the kind gesture in the world of human suffering and deprivation. 33s are often found in caring professions and must guard against being used to further dubious causes which tie human suffering to finance. When operating negatively 33s can be martyrs, depressives and disconsolate individuals.

Suggested professions: Artist, homeopath, union leader, lawyer

MISSING NUMBERS

The missing numbers, also known as karmic numbers or karmic debts, are numbers which indicate uncompleted or unresolved business from a previous existence. Unlike the reservoir numbers, which are a credit from a past life, they represent a debt. They can leave the carrier vulnerable, but once acknowledged, they can be worked on. Karma is the symbolic judgement or correction to be levied for the negative cause and effect of actions in previous lives. The karmic numbers are those which are missing from a name grid. If a carrier's grid is full, with a number or numbers in every square, then he or she has no karmic debt.

For example:

E L I Z A B E T H   K A R E N   G R A N T
5 3 9 8 1 2 5 2 8   2 1 9 5 5   7 9 1 5 2

The missing numbers here are 4 and 6. Refer to the karmic lessons to find out Elizabeth Karen Grant's karmic debts.

The Meaning of the Missing Numbers
To be aware of why something has happened is to be halfway between understanding what has gone wrong and what can be done about it. When the karmic lesson is recognised, much can be done to release conflict and stress.

1

Action or suffer
You will learn this time how important the individual approach to leadership is to you, perhaps through frustration or a series of half-finished projects or tasks when others clean up the trophies that should have been yours, if only you'd stuck it out.

2

Slowly but surely
Clumsiness in word and deed is not a comfortable haven, and the missing 2 will recede into his or her

shell too often after a rebuff or rebuke for insensitivity. They feel loss more than most and their shyness must not be allowed to develop or they may become reclusive.

3
You do count
At some point in a past life there has been a misuse of self-worth, either by the carrier or by those around them. Missing 3s should be well prepared in this lifetime to rectify this injustice and will prevaricate and vacillate till the cows come home on personal progress. Karma never forgets, and living your life through a wild-child partner is helpful but will not suffice entirely. You have to be in it to win it. Come and join the fun – it takes less energy than reticence.

4
Order creates contentment
'What's yours is mine' may have been your motto in a previous life. You may well have been a robber, a highwayman or a fraudster. This time you will be restricted by symbolically building on shifting sands if you repeat the mistakes of the past. If you are prepared to learn the lesson of 4 you may well find yourself in a position of financial trust for an organisation.

5
Relate to life and people, not performance
Life lived constantly in the fast lane is tedious, and that is the official overview of the missing 5. Try it in this lifetime and your path will be strewn with broken relationships, business deals or lost opportunities. How

it affects you this time round will be in your resistance to commitment and taking a chance on things that would be good for you in the long term. Allow yourself to plan and express your opinions clearly.

6
Respond – ability is the road to responsibility
The lesson that it is safe to come home and rest is the message of lesson 6. Multiple marriages simply mean multiple searches for love. Take things slowly and allow yourself to create a loving environment for yourself and those you truly care about. Going out every night is the same as staying in every night: boring.

7
Look, listen and share knowledge
Knowledge is of no value if it's locked away. In a previous life you may have misused the words 'religion' or 'spiritual knowledge'. This time your opinion will be sought and you are advised to give it willingly in order to benefit from the golden gift of communicating with another human being. We employ psychotherapy each and every time we say 'Good morning' to another person. You may enjoy the return gesture.

8
Loyalty breeds good management
A squanderer in a previous life would render the carrier of the 8 to be affluent one minute, destitute the next. In this life, staying away from the betting shop or ridiculously risky deals is recommended. In this lifetime you are able to repair, through prioritising and taking sound advice from people who are experienced and accredited.

9

Giving costs nothing

You may recognise a lack or a much-reduced level of harmony in this lifetime. If this is the case, it's because you never have or make time to watch the flowers grow. Back to the drawing-board, and consider head, heart and gut reactions in everything you do. You are right for you, others are right for themselves; stop trying to be all things to all people. It didn't work in past lives, and it certainly won't work now. Deciding whether being a millionaire in monetary terms is better than being a millionaire in human values might help you focus your path better. Feel as well as deal.

Your Trends

Within a name is a trend, a pattern which is like a tapestry of strength, weakness, restriction or encouragement. Each letter in a name has a single definitive message to which we vibrate and respond whether we choose to or not. It is all part of the identity of you, me, us. We grow into our name just as a child learns to say a name. Mmm, Mim, Mami, Mum, Mummy. Nicknames also stick sometimes because a baby brother could not get his tiny tongue around the real name. With a name it is simple to make a grid and to place in it the number vibration of each letter, in the same way we do a life path grid. As you get more confident, if you have a plethora of 5s, say, you may chose to write 7×5 in the 5 square to show your trends. Personally I still prefer to make a bigger grid and write them all down – that way I keep in touch with the big picture, the feel of what I'm looking at. The grid does not stop at the number inserts, it continues to give insight and information through the vertical, horizontal and diagonal position of the numerical value of the letters.

Every one of you will develop your own method of working once all the facts are there and that is great, because it keeps alive the ever-expanding potential of what else there is to be learned from numerology, whether by chance or by classy mathematics.

Now make a grid, and in each relative square place the number of 1s, 2s, 3s etc contained within the name you are analysing. For example:

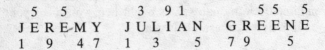

```
   5   5            3  9 1            5 5   5
 J E R E M Y      J U L I A N      G R E E N E
 1   9   4 7      1   3     5      7 9     5
```

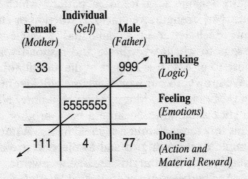

	Individual		
Female (Mother)	*(Self)*	**Male** (Father)	
33		999	**Thinking** (Logic)
	5555555		**Feeling** (Emotions)
111	4	77	**Doing** (Action and Material Reward)

Jeremy Julian Greene, as you can see, has a plethora of 5s in his name, suggesting that he is freedom-seeking, sensitive and may be a bit of a flirt. His trait line of resolve suggests that he is very determined; his trait line of Organisation says that he prefers to be organised but has to put his heart into it, and has noticeable energy levels and good logic. The theatre would suit him as would poetry, or a career involving artistic appreciation such as antique-dealing.

Notice the blanks in his chart? He is missing 2, 4, 6 and 8. These are his karmic lessons. To be aware of them is to protect against them.

```
 1     5  1     1     1     6   9   5
 A N G E L A    M A R T H A    M O R T I M E R
 5 7   3        4   9 2 8      4   9 2 4   9
```

3	6	9999
22	555	8
1111	444	7

The grid is clearly laid out and shows us that Angela has a heavy multiple of 9, but the chart tells the full ability story. She carries an ability number 5 and is energetic, restless at times, with a love of planet earth and the freedom to roam it. Travel would suit her as a profession with music or the theatre a close second. With all the numbers she has as back-up Angela Martha Mortimer's ability to succeed is strong. She has strong traits of logic, organisation, determination and materialism.

Part 4
Making Numerology
work for you

COMPATIBILITY

Lovers, Spouses, Parents, Guardians, Colleagues and Children

We take an enormous gamble with our life paths when we decide to live 'happily ever after' with another human being's life path and reason for being here. In the USA a blood test is required before marriage; perhaps before any marriage anywhere a numerology reading would also be appropriate. With hindsight we can look back and say, 'Boy, oh boy, if I'd known she/he was like that I would never have got involved.'

There are no definite no-nos in numerology, only potentials for a situation to occur, signposts which point to trouble or the vibration to create it. Once we have an awareness of what could be a problem for us or for others close to us, then we can avoid or defuse situations before they get out of hand and respect our own and others' foibles.

We know that two left shoes are not comfortable to wear, and that if someone has an allergy to milk they don't drink milk. Relationships are similar in that there are some people we are never going to settle with, no matter how hard we try.

When we tie the knot or live with someone there are *three* major numerology menus being worked out: in a traditional relationship, the life path of the woman, the life path of the man and the life path of the marriage itself. This also applies to gay relationships or relationships between flatmates. Then there are the respective life paths of and with the children. Whew! Marriage guidance counsellors, treat yourself to a can of spinach.

I referred earlier to the university of family and the lessons we study as a member of that unit. The family would also cover adoptive relationships and substituting a mother and/or father with a guardian is fine.

Let's take an example: mother is a 5, father is an 8 and you are a 2 life path. By adding up the numbers of mother's life path and your own (5 + 2) you create a 7 relationship. This would be a relationship which would have an analytical foundation and would need a lot of understanding from both parties. It will however be a relationship full of information which should be brought to the surface with a strong possibility of the mother being freedom-seeking (5) and the child being a worrier (2), and picking up the debris left by the 5.

The child and the father in this example (2 + 8 = 10) shows the potential for a stable and strong relationship after a struggle, providing the 8 understands the sensitive 2. A leopard can't change its spots, but we can learn to live with the leopard.

Before we look in detail at compatibility potential, a word about relationships between two people with the same life path number. Twins are usually the pairs that cope best with the same life path. We don't marry our twin, and living with someone you mirror can be difficult. So take care, 1 + 1, 2 + 2 and the rest of you.

Compatibles

1 + 1: On the surface this should be a winning set-up provided one golden rule is observed: 1s like to lead, and the old adage 'one captain, one ship' applies here. Define the boundaries from day one. Define who does what and the sky's the limit.

Together they make a 2 relationship: Unity, competitiveness, success with caution. They must recognise two ships and two captains in this combination.

1 + 2: A perfect supply-and-demand relationship. The 1 demands and the 2 willingly supplies. 2s like to be guided, and who better to exert authority than the leading 1.

Together they make a 3 relationship: Demanding with laughs; dominance with acceptance. The 2 must not avoid confrontation with the 1 too often, though.

1 + 3: A middle-of-the-road relationship if the 1 can tolerate the 3's scattiness. Providing the 3 does not overreact to the 1's natural dominance, the 3 could lend welcome lightness to the serious ambition of the 1.

Together they make a 4 relationship: Financially secure with restrictions; safe, sometimes with regrets. A 1 should not push the flirtatious 3 too far. Many other arms would welcome the 3's gaiety.

1 + 4: A clever combination on the face of it. The 1's willingness to try coupled with the 4's need for accuracy and stability would be ideal in the boardroom. In the home, however, the 1 could feel trapped by the 4's constant checking and deliberation on how much better the 1 could have done something. Both are workaholics.

Together they make a 5 relationship: Freedom to cut a

power swathe; loving, with elements of danger. Work romances cannot be ruled out.

1 + 5: These two can be almost too busy to see each other. Very much limelighters, there will not be much time for boredom. Children of such a union may be confused by their parents' behaviour, but life will never be dull with a busy 1 + 5 combination. A theatrical type of family.

Together they made a 6 relationship: Success through action and recognition. A crisis is the only thing that will slow them down.

1 + 6: Two words spring to mind with this combination: creativity and ambition. Providing the 1 acknowledges the 6's creative efforts and the 6 acknowledges the 1's drive, this union has a solid foundation. Both may have to learn to listen to each other.

Together they make a 7 relationship: Don't just know something, say it. Both need to take time to talk, communicate and express freely.

1 + 7: Tread carefully, both. Only when you both realise that the 7 personality needs a lot of space, silence and knowledge, and that the 1 needs fuel for her racing brain, can harmony be found.

Together they make an 8 relationship: A lot of success when they realise both can be right. Family will mean much to them and they may communicate via the children.

1 + 8: A good combination, but some communication problems and misunderstandings. Once you learn to give and take in this relationship the sun can come out from behind the regular cloud.

Together they make a 9 relationship: Surprises, treats and defusing buzzwords to stop lengthy arguments will help this relationship to mature lovingly and peacefully.

1 + 9: The 9's love of glamour and expression plus the 1's daring can make this a dynamic duo. One thing you may have to cope with is the jealousy of your peers for having such a fun-loving union.

Together they make a 10 or 1 relationship: After a bumpy start or separation this can be a vital and loving duo with much to achieve together.

1 + 10: This could be a fraught relationship if 10 feels threatened by the dynamic nature of the true 1. The good news is that if 1 can encourage 10 to shine, confidence can be built. Rare, but miracles do happen.

Together they make a 2 relationship: If the 1 has gained the confidence of the 10 then a late developer has started.

1 + master number 11: This is a good combination providing the 1 is operating positively and the 11 has the space to walk the esoteric path. The poison potential is when either one walks a crooked path.

Together they make a 3 relationship: Laughter should not be far from their busy lives providing they are operating at a positive level. If the bickering starts, this liaison can become extremely tiresome.

1 + master number 22: Dynamite! At its highest potential, the powerful vibration of 1 and master number 22 can be awesome and their combined forces offer them the freedom to experience great wealth and recognition.

Together they make a 5 relationship: Should they try to

take illegal shortcuts that same power can incarcerate them.

1 + master number 33: This can symbolically sum up the business brain (1) and the saint (33). But 33 had better leave time for some fun, or 1 will weary and be off.

Together they make a 7 relationship: With the added creativity and caring of the 33 this pairing may be involved in caring for others professionally.

2 + 2: Kindness oozes from this relationship. 2s, being the nurturers, are like soul-mates. Very much in harmony, they are able to finish each other's sentences or communicate through prolonged silences. Their offspring can often grow up deluded into thinking that the world is a perfect place. 2s are well advised to prepare their offspring for the reality of it.

Together they make a 4 relationship: An orderly and financially prosperous match with kindness a key gesture. They must avoid avoidance of the real world.

2 + 3: Opening a service company together would be a guaranteed success for this match. The vivacious life-loving 3 holds the trump cards in personality stakes and attracting business while the good old reliable 2 grafts away in the background, consolidating and packaging.

Together they make a 5 relationship: Security and fun for this pair, with hospitality and sharing. They both need the tranquillity of the sea or countryside to escape the stresses of life.

2 + 4: There is nothing the 2 and 4 cannot accomplish if they are synchronised. They are capable of being a stylish and conservative pair, languishing in their love of the finer things in life gained through hard work.

Together they make a 6 relationship: Home, social standing and refined order can make this a clockwork marriage union: lunch at lunchtime and tea at teatime.

2 + 5: The 2 may spend a lot of time yawning in the wings watching the 5 take centre stage at every turn. As a couple you may be tempted to change your names to Chalk and Cheese, the two words which describe your make-up perfectly. A brave achievement if you go the distance.

Together they make a 7 relationship: Taking time out for conversation and the 5 not taking the 2 for granted helps enormously.

2 + 6: Cosy describes this liaison. Country walks and drinking hot chocolate by a roaring log fire is their idea of bliss – after they have refurbished their home in à la plush mode. Gaudy lifestyles are not for them; decorum and stability, please.

Together they make an 8 relationship: You and me against the world, babe! The 6 will nurture the 2.

2 + 7: Walking in the Himalayas, opening a New Age bookshop or knitting their own yoghurt suits the 2 and 7 relationship. The 7 can be too esoteric for the 2, though, and 7, you need to include the 2 in your thoughts more.

Together they make a 9 relationship: Potential for great experiences and old-age memories. A bookish or film-loving pairing who have the potential to make their dreams come true.

2 + 8: The caring 2 is a godsend to the resilient and capable 8, offering a haven of peace, love and harmony. The 8 would do well to value the 2's loyalty, diplomacy and considerate nature.

Together they make a 10 or 1 relationship: Loyalty and supportiveness in times of conflict. There are restrictions at some point in this pairing with a potential to win against the odds.

2 + 9: Super hot blend, both at work and at play. They know instinctively how to play each other like an instrument. The 2 anchors the 9's soaring expectations of himself and the 9 is ever grateful. The 9 often has a natural cruel side, and if he does not want to lose the 2, then fidelity and honesty are a must.
Together they make an 11 relationship: A master number union which is highly intuitive and spiritual. When one or both deny the spiritual work they have contracted to do the relationship can be duplicitous and unfulfilling.

2 + master number 10: This is one combination where 2 could be biting the carpet at 10's foolishness in business, his fussy eating habits, or her reticence on the social scene. The long-suffering 2 can make good headway, but only after a can of spinach . . .
Together they make a 3 relationship: This pair will laugh together and may prefer to stay in while in their own country, but let their hair down once a year on their annual holiday.

2 + master number 11: This relationship has a potential for kindness and helpfulness through nurturing and truth. At its worst it could be stressful and fearful.
Together they make a 4 relationship: This is a relationship with a difference. The 2 will encourage the master number 11 to find their spiritual path and develop it, and the honest 11 will stand by the nurturing 2.

2 + master number 22: This combination is a corker in

the master and servant stakes. It might indicate a successful entrepreneur and supportive partner in either business or love.

Together they make a 6 relationship: A willing servant/ master relationship which can work exceedingly well as long as they both follow their life paths in a positive way. This match, whether in work or play, can be gratifyingly creative, both materially and emotionally.

2 + master number 33: A winning combination of family values and a capacity for caring for others.

Together they make an 8 relationship: This relationship thinks on a global scale. With an 8 relationship to manage they are both humanitarian and spiritual. 2 smoothes master number 33's furrowed brow.

3 + 3: The Bonnie and Clyde of numerology – dynamic and dangerous. The only way this combination could work is if one of them had an error in his birth certificate! Try, by all means, but steer clear of illegal situations. Daredevil stunts can go wrong. Watch it!

Together they make a 6 relationship: Creative if used positively, but remember that destructive is the opposite of constructive.

3 + 4: Caring and order is the recipe in this combination. Opening an old folks' home or playing mine hosts in an hotel is right up your life paths. The 4 allows the 3 to be her wild side and the 3 brings laughter and joy to the world of the, at times, too serious 4. However, the solid 4 is not all gloom and brings a welcome stability to the gregarious 3's impulsive streak.

Together they make a 7 relationship: Great friends to have, and they stick like glue to each other in a storm.

3 + 5: Two actors or dramatists in the family can make life fraught. The same applies to the 3 + 5 alliance. It works if one is a comedian and the other an actor, painter or sculptor. Passionate people have wandering passions, so do not be surprised if these rear their head. Both vie for the limelight and often come a cropper by upstaging each other.

Together they make an 8 relationship: Balance is essential. It can work, but only through honesty. See you at the Oscars.

3 + 6: Two 3s make a 6, and this amalgam personifies this partnership. Imagine a whirlwind and two solitary figures the only objects still standing and you've got the pairing of the 3 and the 6. A relationship worth cementing.

Together they make a 9 relationship: Coordinators with a penchant for understanding. Spirited and spiritual, they love grand gestures.

3 + 7: An odd but intriguing liaison, one of the few mixes which can operate after bumpy experiences. Never knowingly undersold in genius, rows, walkouts and making up. Friends of both would do well not to get embroiled in their dramas.

Together they make a 10 or 1 relationship: 7 is the thinker, 3 is the derring-do. Flying crockery is their communication tool.

3 + 8: A 3 is half an 8 when you look at the numbers closely: delightfully successful alchemy. The versatile 3 and the curious 8 know how to pan for gold. They have the potential to remain a couple, as promised to the vicar, 'until DUDP'.

Together they make an 11 relationship: A master number with a special message to give or lesson to learn. More than lucky – synchronic.

3 + 9: 3 × 3 is 9. Running a country house hotel or hosting a chat show is for this showy combination. Perfect in public, they might also successfully run an antiques shop or exclusive deli together.
Together they make a 3 relationship: Fun; frayed tempers in private but they get there in the end.

3 + master number 10: This relationship is either madness, a relationship of convenience, or the 3 sees under the 10's veil of reserve. If the 3 is ambitious and the 10 has brains, behind every successful spouse is an even more ambitious one.
Together they make a 4 relationship: This could be a financially secure union. Providing the 10 develops far enough to keep the cheque book out of the madcap 3's reach for both their sakes.

3 + master number 11: This pair can walk a rocky road together. The 11's need for truth and privacy will clash with the 3's attention-seeking ways. There'll be a lot of irritation if this relationship goes the distance.
Together they make a 5 relationship: The 3 as a dominant partner is urged to consider that they have entered into a freedom-loving relationship with the 11 and must respect the way the 11 exercises his or her freedom.

3 + master number 22: This can work if the 22 holds a high profile in business endeavours. The 22 needs someone to keep confidences, the 3 perhaps cannot.
Together they make a 7 relationship: Both love different limelights: the 3 personal recognition; and the 22

material rewards. Within their 7 relationship much time will be spent searching for these goals. So an appointment system may be the basis for them to meet and remember that they are together.

3 + master number 33: A designer-oriented match with a flair for the big sell. This is a winning combination for two extravagant types, with hearts of gold.

Together they make a 9 relationship: This union can be fraught with duplicity. All that 3 energy and just one relationship to contain it! The 3 has the potential to turn saboteur to the master number 33's crusade. However, at its highest level the 9 relationship they share is dedicated to harmony. This could be a very exciting relationship.

4 + 4: Imagine two accountants marrying and you will be able to sum up the personality of 4 + 4. Working long hours to move to a bigger, better house is their idea of a hobby. Female 4s can be pushy stage mothers. Males can be couch potatoes after giving work – or after work, socialising – their best shot.

Together they make an 8 relationship: They can argue like cat and dog for days, then realise they are on the same side. They often work for the home, not for life.

4 + 5: The successful rock star who marries her manager conjures up a perfect picture of this union. The 5 may get bored with the 4's need for order or profit. When each understands that they both want the good life, the 5 is happy to let 4 create order and megabucks until the cows come home.

Together they make a 9 relationship: The 4 sulks, the 5 seduces, and all's well that ends well in pure silk sheets.

4 + 6: 'If you've got it flaunt it' is the motto of this combination. Never too tired to project themselves as Mr and Mrs, 4 and 6 can be found at the best restaurants and nightclubs simply being seen.

Together they make a 10 or 1 relationship: 'We were the first in our cul-de-sac to have festoon blinds.'

4 + 7: Purity and the search for truth characterise this combination when operating at their highest levels. The universalists of numerology, they could open a spiritual centre, enlighten souls and make millions out of it. Their view is that as long as everybody gets what they want, cost does not come into it.

Together they make an 11 Relationship: Honest and forthright with a smile. We could all take a leaf out of this couple's book if they are living up to their potential. The 4 will lose heart before the 7.

4 + 8: A multiple of the 4, the 8 is the doer and the 4 the worrier in this match. Tension comes in lorryloads, but the gentleness of the 8 allows the 4 to continue in his path of diligence and order. This can be a marriage of convenience with the hope that love will grow. It often does. The health of the 8 can suffer if they squabble too often.

Together they make a 3 relationship: Great ones for a cup of tea and a think. They must guard against change for the sake of change.

4 + 9: The designer and the seamstress are the sum total of the sometimes master-servant 4 and 9 hitch-up. The 9 has the ideas and the 4's orderly ways will make sure everything is done perfectly to please the 9. A very good match if both are operating truthfully. The 9 should note that a major learning curve for him is that every relationship he has is absorbed by the other number. The 9 has to teach and learn about the importance of individuality in all relationships.

Together they make a 4 relationship: Money, money, money. The 4 can get greedy and encroach on the 9's free will after a few years of serving to manipulate.

4 + master number 10: A match made in heaven, or the Bank of England. One thing 4s don't mind doing is putting on the bossy boots. If the 10 is a whinger then the 4 has a bumpier ride, but she wouldn't have it any other way. If or when the 10 finds his feet, then a marvellous business or personal relationship can develop.

Together they make a 5 relationship: Their love of travel can keep them together and working for themselves is even better.

4 + master number 11: A combination of controller and spiritual soul. This relationship can come unstuck through the 4's need to know everything and the 11's capacity for insularity.

Together they make a 6 relatinship: Truth, diligence and the home are the main ingredients of this partnership. A popular couple – their advice is often sought by friends in need. Relaxation is an afternoon at an art gallery.

4 + master number 22: A corporate image dream or a jealousy-ridden liaison. If both are ambitious it can be a moderately good union; if the 22 is duplicitous the 4 will spend a lifetime trying to find him out.

Together they make an 8 relationship: This is a hard working duo who may verge on workaholism. Children of this 8 union will be driven hard to succeed. This pairing feel that only hard work creates success.

4 + master number 33: A combination of the saver, the 4, and the giver, the 33. The 33's need to heal the world might annoy the 4 beyond the pale.

Together they make a 10 or 1 relationship: The energy in this union may leave the rest of us breathless, but they do get things done, if operating as a 1. Don't expect to leave a dinner party in this home without having sponsored a charity walk, swim, or decathlon. As a 10, their bickering can be embarrassing and wearing to others.

5 + 5: Say goodnight now, for both your sakes! You both want thrills and you want them now. In a relationship one 5 will flirt, the other will react angrily and the bewildered innocent third party will come off worse, leaving a sour aftertaste.

Together they make a 10 or 1 relationship: Never do a joint parachute jump with each other!

5 + 6: Both can be moody and petulant. The 5 needs constant stimulus, and why not, after all, she is a 5. The creative, snobbish and community-oriented 6 can find the 5 passionate, wearing but highly mesmeric. They may benefit from a counsellor to keep on track.

Together they make an 11 relationship: Intuitive but irregular. The 6 shouts 'Rent', the 5 cries 'Spent!'

5 + 7: The social butterfly 5 is capable of putting the studious and spiritual 7 in a straitjacket. The 7 has the capability to throttle the 5. While the 7 is struggling with the universal why, the 5 has a turban round her head telling fortunes accurately at the end of a pier for a laugh. Try if you will, but the best that can happen is that the 5 can show the 7 how to boogie.

Together they make a 3 relationship: A lot of laughs with plenty of gaffs. Travelling keeps the 5 a happy international shopper and the 7 informed.

5 + 8: Dreamer plus schemer plus workers make millionaires. Concorde is their idea of local transport, so dynamic is the potential of this pair. The 8 will make a loving and stable partner for the 5, while the 5 fulfils the 8's sexual desires.

Together they make a 4 relationship: 'We won't waste a minute, and if we do we'll work twice as hard next time.'

5 + 9: Laughter is the catalyst in this bond. If you want to make it, at least make it funny. Spend, spend, spend is their second motto – however, credit where it's due, providing they earn, earn, earn first. The best part of breaking up is making up, but how they ever got together in the first place . . .

Together they make a 5 relationship: Sailing close to the wind at times keeps them interested. All bills are red to them.

5 + master number 10: 'Oh get on with it!' the gregarious 5 may cry. But the 10 admires the 5's drive and may pick up the fun factor quite quickly, if willing. If the 10 insists on moping the 5 will seek out other social outlets and leave the 10 to the potting shed or embroidery by the fireside.

Together they make a 6 relationship: The home may be the only place they exchange words. 5 loves to be doing, 10 to be worrying. Although if or when the 10 comes out of their shell, watch them at the sixties disco night. Kipper tie and flares out of the loft . . .

5 + master number 11: Good for compassion and

understanding and romantic interludes and gestures. The 5 may be too dramatic for the 11 and the 11 may also tire of the 5's over-the-top analysis of everything.

Together they make a 7 relationship: The love of home and travel could conflict more than often and this couple need to be sure of the ground rules before embarking on a long-term commitment. It can work if they respect that they have different needs.

5 + master number 22: This couple may experience more offs than ons in their courtship, but with a bit of fine tuning they can enjoy a moderate to good relationship.

Together they make a 9 relationship: Two people who really enjoy life and the entertaining skills of the 5 enhance the 22's ambitious corporate attitude. Their 9 relationship is durable and forward-thinking.

5 + master number 33: You have to learn how to argue constructively. The 33 can be preoccupied and hypersensitive while the 5 barges on regardless. You could agree on a 'defuse word' for either partner to use to indicate 'that's far enough on this topic'.

Together they make a 2 or master number 11 relationship: If working as a 2 vibration, to find this couple working abroad in a voluntary organisation would be no surprise. As an 11 they are great defenders of the truth and may work for an embassy abroad.

6 + 6: Copies of *Country Life* and *Tatler* are never far from the 6 + 6's dreamy gaze. Walking around another stately home, checking out how they should be living, is their idea of a good day out – then it's back home to replan the sitting room. They hate being wrong and stick together like toffee on a blanket in public.

Together they make a 3 relationship: Welcome to our home, but wipe your feet. Fish knives for fish, sherry glasses for sherry, they make you believe they are more royal than the royals.

6 + 7: Imagine someone continuing to read the newspaper while you tell them you've split the atom again, and you've got the 6 + 7 at their worst. At their best they are happy to meet each other in bed after all their evening classes and use pottery-speak and navigation-class language as foreplay.

Together they make a 4 relationship: Fruitful in converting hobbies into profit. They might make another couple very happy . . .

6 + 8: Gearbox and gearstick is the best metaphor for 6 + 8. One is not much use without the other. A loving and caring long-distance runner, this one. Friends can start saving up for the golden wedding present now.

Together they make a 5 relationship: Equal input equals double dividends. A true couple, and if divorce is considered think very carefully before ditching this partnership.

6 + 9: Like 3 + 9 but more frothy. This pair are capable of communicating telepathically. One senses the other's pain and responds automatically to defuse potentially harmful confrontation. A match made in heaven. If they are supportive of each other in the right way they are usually the cornerstone of their respective families.

Together they make a 6 relationship: 6 offers welcoming style, 9 offers grandeur. This would also apply in their treatment of others: if 9 needs to impress the boss he invites him home to meet 6.

6 + master number 10: A nice combination, with the caring touch from the 6 whose patience can create something out of the wilderness. The 6 will invite the committee back for a night-cap and the 10 will either have tea and cakes laid on or be sulking in the shed.
Together they make a 7 relationship: A lot of understanding is needed in this liaison with the 6 playing analyst and the 10 on the couch.

6 + master number 11: This pairing doesn't go out much, preferring the cosiness of the hearth to the razzmatazz. The 2 would be well advised, though, to watch out for the 6's bohemian streak and insist that she expresses herself through art or communication skills.
Together they make an 8 relationship: A great sense of family and a comfortable home are the prerequisites of this 8 relationship. Sometimes snobs, they do enjoy being admired and quite rightly because they work hard for it.

6 + master number 22: A creative and ambitious match who can reach Hollywood proportions in their zest for life. A most expressive pairing, they welcome others into their environment.
Together they make a 1 relationship: It would be no surprise if 6 was the boss's daughter or son. Both numbers know from a very early age what they want and where they are going.

6 + master number 33: Potentially a match made in heaven. They may well find themselves organising their community and the welfare of others. To find two medical workers in this configuration would not be unusual.

Together they make a 3 relationship: This is a pairing of soulmates. They are curious about everything and everyone, often bordering on nosiness. In their 3 relationship they can be hypercritical of 'lesser' mortals.

7 + 7: An eccentric, extreme combination. You are the type who forget to eat for a couple of days because you are engrossed in translating an illuminated manuscript or ironing the Dead Sea Scrolls. You often find mundane things like paying the gas, electricity or water rates an ordeal, but climbing K2 relaxing. Both hoarders, you may move to a bigger house because the rooms are overflowing.

Together they make a 5 relationship: And get away with breaking most relationship rules because they trust each other implicitly, often from miles apart. Not party animals.

7 + 8: The 7 drives the practical 8 up the wall at times, but the 8 is on a long fuse. The information-filled 7 will fascinate the 8 with the most interesting of fine detail. The 8, a status-enjoying number, is proud of such a catch and of the academic status conferred on him by the 7 without him ever having to open a book.

Together they make a 6 relationship: The forgiving 8 is generally tolerant of the swotty 7. When the 7 worries about the earth's axis shifting the 8 will make a cup of cocoa and put on his fishing by numbers video.

7 + 9: Quite a magical combination in numerology. Stonehenge is a perfect place to honeymoon for this contented pair, and opening a vegetarian restaurant with a free astrological reading on orders over £10 would marry the flair of the 9 and the environmental awareness of the 7.

Together they make a 7 relationship: An extremely informed and spiritual couple. Los Angeles or Glaston-bury? Who cares as long as it's near an antiques shop, a crystals shop or on a ley-line.

7 + master number 10: This pair may communicate through the written word. Either books or via lawyer. The knowledgeable 7 must resist trying to give the 10 too many details or examples and the 10 could help by remembering that the 7 is only trying to help. Once they get past this barrier, the potential for a positive 10 and a positive 7 is a learned relationship.

Together they make an 8 relationship: Get through the first five years and the reward can be magical. As an 8 relationship they can create a good family foundation with success a bit later than most.

7 + master number 11: So much knowledge, so much light. This relationship at its highest potential is about understanding. The 7 seeks; the 11 shines.

Together they make a 9 relationship: Harmony, trust and isolation. This couple play their cards close to the chest.

7 + master number 22: As a business pair this is inventor (7) + investor (22). They have the potential to analyse a market and scoop up. If operating negatively the 7 can be aloof, moody and closed, and the 22 downright duplicitous.

Together they make a master number 11 relationship: They have a potential for working out life's little intrica-cies.

7 + master number 33: Priest and nun. This pair are spiritual, giving and full of resolve when under pressure – see the 7's clarity of mind, and the 33's energy and sense of justice is commendable. However if operating negatively they can be disillusioned if they haven't gone into the fine print in detail.

Together they make a 4 relationship: The chances are that this is a good match.

8 + 8: These two are victims of circumstance on occasion. Things happen around 8s. Unless you are both prepared for an extremely exciting lifestyle you should find more sober partners. You might also have met in a crisis situation.

Together they make a 7 relationship: Live and let live, you two: kissing and bliss instead of castigating for days. Making up is of great benefit to you.

8 + 9: A neat combination of determination, flair and guts. A popular pair who encourage growth in each other. The 8 is the worker and facilitator of the duo and the 9 allows them to proceed unhindered while 8 saves the world. The 8 can tire of the 9's head in the cloud approach, but on the whole they are akin to gin and tonic – they go well together.

Together they make an 8 relationship: The 8 is the leader and a source of inspiration for the 9's boundless energy. They do excellent teamwork and their bike 'n sidecar mentality is successful.

8 + master number 10: The 8 usually has the patience of a saint, and the eagerness of the 10 to please a nurturing 8 is usually touching. The 8 is considered the power behind the throne and the 10 is generally grateful for the 8's loyal support.

Together they make a 9 relationship: Both enjoy pleasing surroundings and have eclectic taste in art and antiques. The 8 will normally choose or direct the 10 towards a new image in clothes, which usually works.

8 + master number 11: Provides a close family environment which gives security to all within that family. Good finances are a potential with this match, and it is likely that children will take over the family business.

Together they make a 1 relationship: This is a very clear-cut relationship – the 8 has ambition; the 11 has clarity and vision. When operating positively they make a splendid 1 vibration.

8 + master number 22: These two can reach great heights together and the 22 can benefit from the 8's intuition on all levels. The 8 will feel secure in the 22's meteoric professional rise.

Together they make a 3 relationship: Like the 8 + master number 11 relationship, this is a vibrant, strong partnership. Both parties have their feet firmly on the ground and the money in the bank.

8 + master number 33: The home will be the focus of this match. This combination is one of the best balanced in numerology because of the loving and sure nature of the 8 and the caring, creative nature of the 33.

Together they make a 5 relationship: A lot of tension in this relationship with the 8 often angry at how the 33's time is easily hi-jacked by needy others. They create a 5 vibration of respecting freedom and would be encouraged to escape either on holiday or by unhooking the phone.

9 + 9: Perfectionists in the understanding of the meaning of life. He brings her flowers regularly, she leaves him notes under his pillow. Reality can die for this pair, but never romance. They may tire of constant sweetness as both crave attention and one of them may choose to introduce a souring contrast by having affairs.

Together they make a 9 relationship: Keeping in touch with reality is a lesson for them this time round, and of course the 9 is always absorbed by the other number, a quirk of fact of number. In this pairing, one of them could hold a destructive streak if the other is progressing too fast.

9 + master number 10: The 10 can be lost until the 9 comes on the scene and then things start to happen. Because of the 9's ability to make his dreams come true the 10 can only be affected to their advantage. This pair can go far and being at opposite ends of the numerological scale prove that opposites can attract.

Together they make a master number 10 or a glorious 1 relationship: A betting person would put money on this match as the potential for many enjoyable journeys and experiences.

9 + master number 11: When harmony and insight get together the result is an identikit of a lovely relationship. This combination would also make for a good business partnership or good colleagues.

Together they make a 2 or master number 11 relationship: This is an odd match in that the 11 doesn't actually trust the 9 completely. 9's charming manner can be cloying in contrast with the directness of 11.

9 + master number 22: A hotchpotch, this one. Both could symbolically walk towards each other and miss each other by a mile. In short it can work, but needs patience. The 9's flirting will take the 22 a bit of getting used to.

Together they make a 4 relationship: The 4 relationship made by 9 and 22 creates order where there is chaos, and tranquillity where there is strife. The 9 dislikes friction but often attracts it and the 4 vibration offers only two choices: order or chaos.

9 + master number 33: 3×3 is 9, so wherever you turn in this relationship there is a twinning, an indivisible bond. This relationship is the envy of your peers and a good advertisement for marriage!

Together they make a 6 relationship: The master number 33 can often be too slow for the 9, but the 9 can learn much from the 33's devotion. Their 6 partnership offers them recognition in the community and both have much to offer as a team this time round.

Master numbers 10 + 10: Think very carefully before investing in this one. It can veer between two defeatists or two winners. Perhaps it would be advisable to establish very early on what you both desire from this relationship rather than muddle into the depths of despair and struggle.

Together they make a 2 relationship: Warm and loving if it works; a miserable struggle if it doesn't.

Master numbers 10 + 11: Interesting this one as the patient 11 can enlighten the 10's gloom and show them both the way forward. If the 11 is operating negatively they will take advantage of the 10's struggle and either leave or milk it until they've taken all.

Together they make a 3 relationship: On the bright side, they will have ups and downs but if, or when, the 10 strengthens then life can go on. There could be too much strife for both of them if things get out of hand. In fact each might find greater happiness with someone else . . .

Master numbers 10 + 22: Strangely enough this could work if the 10 is willing to learn. I do not suggest however that they work together. 22 is too ambitious to tolerate anything less than top speed. This is a good marriage partnership where one succeeds and the other serves. Woe betide the 22 when the 10 develops into a 1 though. Expect fireworks.
Together they make a 5 relationship: Dramatic, never dull, and definitely inventive.

Master numbers 10 + 33: I cannot imagine anything more miserable than a negative master number 10 and a negative master number 33. Defeatist and martyr, what a combination. However, a developed 10 to a 1 and a courageous, humanitarian 33 can exist and work together beautifully. The positive 10/1 can keep the fund-raising going while the 33 saves the world.
Together they make a 7 relationship: A good potential for a spiritual quest together. Soulmates maybe? One thing is for sure, it had better be positive.

Master numbers 11 + 11: This combination is here this time round to undertake great works of enlightenment and the spreading of truth. Both people would work well in complementary healing work, as documentary makers or as civil rights workers.
Together they make a master number 22 or a 4 relationship: I hope for their sakes they are both Buddhists for this has the potential to be a very spiritual union. Both are interested in the higher mind, and can be quite

solitary within a relationship, whether it is professional or personal. The 22 vibration offers them a successful journey, provided they walk in the light.

Master numbers 11 + 22: Can reach the stars and beyond – not for them a life of struggle. The 22's feet are kept on the ground by the advice of the 11 and the 11 is proud of the 22's achievement as well as his own.
Together they make a master number 33 or a 6 relationship: As a master number 33 this couple may well find themselves looking after relatives or having their time restricted. They must strive to keep their individuality at all costs, but they will be expected to serve others as part of their master number life paths and relationship path.

Master numbers 11 + 33: The 11 will light a candle for the 33 when all seems lost in the world of human caring. Then it's everyone back on the coach and into action again. A relationship in which love and understanding are abundant.
Together they make an 8 relationship: This pair must avoid martyrdom, when they do they can devote adequate time to home, family and get to know that word fun.

Master numbers 22 + 22: I do not want to be around when the sparks fly here! It is a tense but rewarding relationship – providing they meet at airports. Even their sandwiches are designer, darling. They use words like genre, aesthetic and absolutely frequently. A mesmeric mix.
Together they make an 8 relationship: This could have been Margaret Thatcher and Robert Maxwell – both are here to learn how to respect power and the 8 relationship

makes for a close-knit family. Power and ambition is the foundation of this union.

Master numbers 22 + 33: A stylish relationship provided the 22 tells the truth and the 33 does not become a martyr. They have the potential to be a celebrity couple, and that can also apply to Acacia Avenue. Theirs is that one house in every street that is over the top or stunning. **Together they make a master number 10 or a 1 relationship:** 33 does good works and 22 provides the manor house in which they live. In an established village they *are* the village.

Master numbers 33 + 33: Get out either the tissues, the pottery kiln or the Red Cross trucks. There are no half measures in this match. These two are either whingers, extremely creative or relief workers in war zones. The children of this couple may have to book an appointment to meet their parents.
Together they make a 3 relationship: This couple has a potential to be burdened by the sins of the world. They cannot resist colonising, rehabilitating and sometimes forcing their beliefs down the throats of others. On the plus side, two 33s have probably saved the planet on more than one occasion. Their 3 relationship offers humour and maybe an inclination to laugh at their more serious side.

The analysis of compatability through numerology does not, of course, apply solely to romantic or family relationships. It can be very helpful in understanding our relationships with any individual. To illustrate this point, let's look in detail at two cases from my own experience where numerology was used effectively to deal with problems arising at school and at work.

Case Study 1

To recognise when a child in your care is in trouble or distress, whether you are a parent, guardian, granny or teacher, is to be half-way to helping that relatively new human solve the problem. To act upon it and help the child keeps society acceptable. Numerology is a fine tool in the analysis of potential weaknesses and strengths, and encouraging the child to realise the potential of beneficial change is most rewarding for helper and child.

I met a ten-year-old child who had gone beyond the limits of human endurance as a victim of school bullying. He was brought along by his huffing and puffing businesswoman mother, and as it transpired, had a father who was much too busy travelling the world for his company to attend any sessions with his son and therefore attempted to direct the meetings by regular phone calls. The child's beautiful face bore the dark rings of insomnia and stress below the eyes and he had recently started vomiting before each potentially terrifying school day. He had been checked by his GP, who concluded that the vomiting was a psychosomatic cry from the child that he 'could not stomach something in his life'.

During our meetings we opened up David's potential to empower himself with useful and constructive knowledge by analysing the main bully's date of birth. This took careful handling on my part, and required a total respect for David's fear of such perpetrators of terror. We couldn't stop the bully, simply because he was not in the room, or more importantly, he was not available or ready for change. But by raising David's self-esteem, together we reactivated his options for changing his own response to the bully.

I had many factors to work on, a major one being David's mother, who cut across any answer I needed from the boy himself. That necessitated her being tactfully excluded from the sessions.

One part of his treatment was a task for him: to find out the date of birth of the bully, and through careful detective work this was discovered. I then constructed a chart for the offender and one for the young patient. The results were intriguing. David's date of birth was 23/8/1983 (life path 7), and the bully's 15/5/1983 (life path 5).

David's Chart

Female *(Mother)*	Individual *(Self)*	Male *(Father)*	
33		9	**Thinking** *(Logic)*
2		88	**Feeling** *(Emotions)*
1			**Doing** *(Action and Material Reward)*

Bully's Chart

| | Individual | | |
Female *(Mother)*	*(Self)*	Male *(Father)*	
3		9	**Thinking** *(Logic)*
	55	8	**Feeling** *(Emotions)*
11			**Doing** *(Action and Material Reward)*

The two 5s in the bully's chart show that his potential to overstep the drama lines borders on the dangerous if operating negatively. It also indicates that he has the ability to charm (or lie) his way out of trouble or admonishment. He has a strong trait line of resolve, and here the golden rule of numerology must be remembered: with every potential for positive meaning there is the equal potential for negative. So his line of resolve can help him get things done or destroy others.

The 3 and 8 in his chart show that the bully is intuitive and can assess very quickly. In its negative role, this ability could be used to pick up others' weaknesses and play on them. If we look at the patient's chart we see that he too has a 3 and two 8s, indicating that he has the potential to frustrate the bully. This factor gave the patient a morale-boost.

By looking at trait lines you can see that David's chart

betrays the tell-tale sign of something missing: note the gap in the individual plane. The chart suggests that the parents, his role models, may knowingly or unwittingly leave him feeling isolated and override his opinions and perhaps ignore his needs. This in turn could leave him unsure of himself and vulnerable in public to figures in authority or those simulating authority – in his case bullies. His chart also indicates a separation or distancing from the father (note the gap in the emotions plane between 1 and 9). This was confirmed by the fact that the mother's business took up her time, and by the dismissiveness of the father who, in his ignorance and frustration, thought all he had to do was throw money at the problem and all would be well.

David's chart also shows that the boy is a good organiser (female column). He and the bully both prefer activity. David has two 8s, indicating that he will witness, experience and deal with many things in life.

What appealed to David was the fact that he was more organised than Bully Billy and that he, as a life path 7, was probably more knowledgeable. On the learning-curve side, David had a major lesson to learn about believing in himself (see the self-esteem trait line).

Bully Billy is a life path 5 and needs to be aware of the importance of freedom. That knowledge would incorporate acknowledging others' rights of freedom. He's in a learning curve of defeatism masked by bravado, the two 5s of excessive emotion in the individual plane.

David, through some excellent work on himself, used the knowledge of the gems he carried in his birthdate numbers very bravely, choosing to tell his adversary when he caught him on his own on the way to school one day that Billy was scared of his freedom, and that he was wasting his life.

This conversation was not instigated by me at all. David, through the many questions he asked about numerology and the bully's numbers, worked out that Billy was a person who behaved the way he did because he was hurt. All nice and cosy, you might say, but the way David proceeded to handle the situation was admirable. He invited Billy to meet him behind the bus shelter, saying that he would only be there if Billy had the courage to come alone. Naturally, Billy refused – it's no use being a bully if you don't have an audience. David told him he understood that he was scared and walked away. The bully protested and insisted on bringing a friend, but David stuck to his guns and refused. Billy had to accept the offer and the great success of the whole episode was that David got him to come alone.

David took a computer game to the rendezvous and, rather than offering the bully a fight, which the boy expected, he challenged him to a game on the screen to settle their differences. David told me they had such a good time that they continued for over an hour, and were late home. He also added that although they are not friends, they have a common ground now, the space behind the bus shelter, and non-violent win-or-lose communication through the game.

David succeeded in activating the wisdom of the two 8s in his chart and acknowledging that he had to experience a lot of things in his life, so he'd better start now. He also knew that by adding his life path and

Billy's we create a 12/3 relationship, 3 being the number of spontaneity, lightheartedness and action.

We could not alter his parents' dismissiveness, although I pointed it out to them clearly, but David felt he could alter his response to the bully, and achieved that. I am very proud of him. The moral of this tale is that children understand games better than we do and can utilise numerology in their own way.

Case Study 2

Do you love your job but just can't click with your boss any more? When this happens a job which you both thought you wanted to do as a team suddenly changes into a daily ordeal. More than likely it's a conflict of numbers or learning curves, and the good news is that it may well be only temporary and resolvable. Belligerence, spitefulness and sarcasm are often used as defence mechanisms in such atmospheres, and even though these metaphoric walls can defend us, we must also remember that such walls also define prisons, and the place where we volunteer eight hours of our time a day in order to earn a living can be a minefield of stress and eroded self-esteem.

By carefully comparing the numbers of each person and analysing the path you are both following much understanding can be gained and progress made. You may not be able to convince anyone else of the importance of numerology, but if you believe it can help you then you can make situations work for you through understanding what is actually happening.

Kay came to see me in a distressed state and put all her troubles down to Jay, her 'recently nasty boss' of six years. I looked at the plusses in their working relationship and wondered why they had both been battling for so long.

The facts were as follows: Jay interviewed her and selected her out of fourteen applicants. Obviously this told me that he preferred and chose her abilities and presentability above those of thirteen other candidates. Kay liked Jay at all three interviews and looked forward to working with him. They made a good office team, and Kay worked overtime on many occasions without being asked. Jay was always appreciative.

Yet after three years of reasonable harmony in a financially stable company Jay suddenly became critical and sarcastic, speaking to Kay in a manner which exceeded the boundaries of a healthy employer/employee relationship.

Jay's date of birth was 21/7/1956 (life path 31/4); Kay's was 15/9/1976 (life path 38/11). At the end of 1989, when things were at their worst, Jay was in a personal year 10/1, and Kay in a personal year 42/6. By adding their respective years we calculated a joint personal year, 7, which shows they shared the need to analyse what they really wanted and needed, or what was blocking the present. It is no surprise, then, that they experienced such a breakdown in communications: they were both searching for a solution but had a battle instead.

Kay's Chart

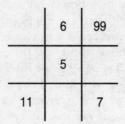

	6	99
	5	
11		7

Jay's Chart

	6	9
2	5	
11		7

Now just look at these almost identical charts – Kay's has one extra 9, and of course they have very different life path numbers. Nevertheless, they have a lot in common.

178

Jay's life path is 4, one of order and hard work if operating positively, or chaos and hypercriticism if operating negatively. Kay's life path is master number 11, intuitive, psychic and sensitive if operating positively; complaining and over-sensitive if not.

Both are determined (trait line of resolve), knowledgeable (the 7), well-balanced (each north, south and diagonal trait line has at least two numbers to fill the squares). So what went wrong?

Jay, an engineer, became a father for the third time at the age of thirty. He made it known at the time of his wife's pregnancy that he was not thrilled about the birth of another child. He had been offered a contract for two years, *en famille*, on a prestigious project in Saudi Arabia and had had to forgo the professional promotion because of the imminent birth of his child.

Kay and I worked out the pattern through the numbers and her memory of what was going on around that time. This was in 1986, when he was in a personal year 7, a year when he had to prepare through deep personal analysis for the success of the following magical personal year 8, the year of accolade and success. It appears that Jay felt trapped professionally by the birth of another child, and as a result the marriage was going through a bad patch.

So, you might be forgiven for saying, that's simply a guy grumpy at his family versus career situation. OK, you can leave it at that, and continue to battle with his grumpiness, or you can work out the potential of the situation. Kay had no interest in his private life, but she had a vested interest in how it affected her.

The potential of the now for Kay was that Jay was in a personal year 10, a master number year of new

179

beginnings, of success after a struggle. Kay was in the very creative personal year 6, and more able to assert her right to control and reform what happened to her, and as we've seen, as a unit of communication they were currently experiencing a personal year 7.

Something had to be done. Kay understood that her boss did not have the insight she had gained through our numerology session and decided she would approach him to discuss what had gone wrong in their relationship.

Ten days later she called me and was disappointed but not surprised that she had been sarcastically rejected by him. She pointed out that he was unusually defensive. I remarked: 'Methinks he doth protest too much.' She was quiet for a moment, and then asked for a copy of the double chart as a gift for him, joking that she had nothing left to lose. Even if she had to leave her well-paid job at least she could use the goodwill gesture of the chart analysis as proof at any unfair dismissal tribunal that she had tried everything in her power to rectify the situation. I sent the chart and heard no more for almost three weeks. But a surprise lay in store: I had a call from Jay who thanked me for the chart and wondered if he and his wife could have one done. I also took down the details of the baby he hadn't wanted initially, and slipped in a freebie chart for this innocent little person who had joined them in the university of family. The healing power of numerology is endless.

NUMEROLOGY IN HISTORY

The Numerical Vibrations of Global Events

Rather than overplay the sometimes spectacular history of numbers, allow the numbers in history to help you to relate to the patterns within the subject; the importance of numbers to historians, if only to identify periods of history for reference and teaching. Numerology highlights patterns and similarities which are too interesting to gloss over. It is most important for the student to remember that not all carriers of numbers use them in a positive way, so any number vibration must be viewed from both aspects.

Below are a few examples correlated into life path vibrations of particular significant events to encourage the reader to be aware of the natural patterns into which lives and events fall. Everything has a purpose and a meaning. It is a reminder that everything is number.

10
The master number of success after a great struggle and obstacles
8/11/1961 = 10: Negotiations for Britain's entry into the Common Market begin. 10 is the master number of success after an arduous struggle (oh, really?).

11
The master number of light and truth
25/8/1940 = 29; 2 + 9 = 11: Britain began bombing Germany. The first of the 11's to pepper the Second World War. The master number 11 is the number of insight and shining light where darkness threatens. The opposite of positive 11 is uncaring, shady and devious. Notice how sometimes World War II is written like an 11?
13/8/1961 = 29; 2 + 9 = 11: Soviet Berlin was walled off from the Western Sector. The master number of the psychic, which, when operating positively, throws light

and awareness on facts. When operating negatively it conceals, secretes and covers truth.

11/10/1969 = 38; 3 + 8 = 11: The Soviet spacecraft Soyuz was launched and became the first to undertake welding in space. On 31/7/1969 (= 38; 3 + 8 = 11) Mariner 6 took photographs of Mars which were transmitted back to earth for televising.

22

The master number of monumental success through organisation

14/11/1941 = 22: The Ark Royal was sunk. The master number 22 is at best orderly, organised and capable of great things. At worst it is despotic, terrorising and the number of great loss.

23/10/1942 = 22: The battle of El Alamein was instigated. 22, the number of capability, courage and power; if negative, malevolent.

3/10/1962 = 22: A US astronaut joined the 6 orbit flight. 22, the master number of great things being possible.

33

The master number of the healer, the creator and the pacifist – the opposite if used negatively

6/8/1945 = 33: The first use of the atomic bomb on Hiroshima. The master number 33 is the most painful of numbers to carry. Its vibration is the healer; if negatively used, the destroyer.

1

The number of leadership and logistics

2/3/1958 = 10; 1 + 0 = 1: Sir Vivian Fuchs led the first expedition across the Arctic, travelling 2,200 miles in 99 days.

2
The number of home, family and supporting
1/1/1962 = 20; 2 + 0 = 2: Western Samoa becomes independent. This typifies the caring home-base nature of 2.

3
The number of spontaneity and joy
2/9/1945 = 30; 3 + 0 = 3: The end of the Second World War. 3, the number of the Trinity: three wise men; we officiate in triplicate; the sun, the moon and the stars; the number of triangle.

4
The number of order, diligence and accountability
16/11/1957 = 31; 3 + 1 = 4: Russia announces construction of 'scientific cities' in Siberia, which will consist of twelve institutes.

5
The number of freedom, and the respecting of it
4/4/1968 = 32; 3 + 2 = 5: Martin Luther King was assassinated in Memphis, Tennessee. 5, the number of freedom, drama, daring and, when exercised negatively, excessive waste and shock.

6
The number of creative endeavour and correcting destruction
6/12/1941 = 24; 2 + 4 = 6: The Japanese attacked Pearl

Harbor. 6, the number of creativity when operating positively and destruction when the negative aspect is employed.

7
The number of the teacher, seeker of knowledge
3/9/1939 = 34; 3 + 4 = 7: The Second World War broke out at 11 a.m. The positive meaning of 7 is analysis. The opposite or negative meaning is random.

8
The number of balancing heaven and earth, spirit and materialism
17/3/1959 = 35; 3 + 5 = 8: The Dalai Lama of Tibet fled to India. 8, the number of balancing the higher mind and the material side of life. His escape could be seen as a monumental success today, for it freed the Dalai Lama to work tirelessly to peacefully raise awareness of Tibet's plight.
21/7/1969 = 35; 3 + 5 = 8: Neil Armstrong and Buzz Aldrin became the first two humans on the moon at 3.56 a.m. British Summer Time. Now that is a success! Splashdown was on 24/7/1969 (= 38, or master number 11).
22/11/1964 = 26: 2 + 6 = 8: John F. Kennedy was shot in Dallas. 8, the number of balancing the spiritual and the material if operating positively; when negatively employed the number of baseness and duplicity. Kennedy was the 35th (3 + 5 = 8) president of the USA.
5/6/1969 = 35; 3 + 5 + 8: Robert Kennedy was shot dead in Los Angeles, assassinated, like his brother Jack, on an 8 vibration.

9

The number of bringing together, harmonising
7/3/1970 = 27; 2 + 7 = 9: There was a total eclipse of the sun in Mexico.

HOUSE AND WORK NUMBER VIBRATIONS

Numerology is about vibration as well as personality and potential, and how many houses have you entered and found harmonious, disruptive or creepy? We can learn more about the home we live in or intend to live in by analysing the number and the name of the street, road or avenue.

We can look at a house and its owner or occupier and feel that the house makes a statement about them. If we can judge that quickly, then there's definitely more to come with the number or area identifier.

The number is the premier vibration; however, if the house in question is known as Rose Cottage, then the vibration of the letters contained within that name are the premier vibration. The street name is not the main issue. When calculating the numerical value of the house, use only the name, number, and name of road. The words 'street', 'avenue', 'road', 'terrace' or whatever can be ignored. For example:

```
3 6 6    W I N D M I L L    H I L L    (STREET)
3 6 6    5 9 5 4 4 9 3 3    8 9 3 3      = 80/8
15/6                        65/11
```

The premier vibration is 15/6, and the importance of this as a family/home base would be excellent. It may be in an enviable position and unusual in decor or architecture. Each individual occupant's life path and/or psyche number can be analysed with the house number, and the occupying residents collectively and then reduced to a single digit or master number life path. The persona number, however, may produce a clash of vibrations, for then the 'keeping up with the Jones's' syndrome can come into play. It works in the same way as a compatibility assessment.

There would also be the potential for a lightening of a load or the brightening up of a lifestyle with the illuminating and understanding master number 11 vibration of the street name only.

The lesson of living at or with the full number, 8, would be balancing the spiritual and the material. It also has the potential to be a lucky property. Should it be a place of work or a business address, then the ability number should be analysed or compared to it. Many interesting things would happen in this place, and the occupier should be prepared for this. It may even be haunted.

A major factor in any numerology analysis is when the person, property, event or whatever is born or to be born. With a property the date it was built is its life path. So, if you have the builders' certificate or the completion date, that would constitute the life path of the property, and with that information you could proceed to calculate the ability, persona and the psyche of the place you are intending to be closely associated with.

This is particularly helpful if you have had a bad deal or made a bad move in previous abodes. At least you are taking some responsibility for not making the same mistake again. You may also do the house number vibration of the properties on either side, if applicable.

Remember, when you buy the house, you also buy the neighbours.

Car numbers, too, can be analysed. Simply add together the numbers of the registration plate along with the numerical value of the letters contained within it.

A special point on workplace numbers. The sick building syndrome is a problem of modern times and has an interesting factor in that not all employees in the building are affected. If a workplace affects you then treat yourself to the analysis of the building which may be jarring your life path, persona, psyche or ability vibration, not forgetting to ask yourself honestly if you should be doing that job anyway! Don't blame the building vibration when you are denying your ability or life path.

THE COMPOUND NUMBERS

The penultimate number in a reduction, e.g. 27, when $2 + 7 = 9$, is of great importance as a sub-lesson before the carrier reaches his or her ultimate life path number. These double-digit calculations are known as the compound number. As we all know, a compound is something which is made up of differing elements or, in the compound number's case, different values and vibrations. The compound numbers and their meanings are valuable in analysing and providing extra information about the vibrations of names, addresses, houses, cars, telephone numbers, credit account numbers and so on.

The compound numbers begin at 10, and although several numerology examples indicate that they are repetitive after a certain number it is important to note the order in which they fall. 31 and 13, for example, contain the same numbers but the first digits are miles apart in meaning. The first digit will give the premier vibration and the second the secondary vibration. So in 13 the premier vibration is 1, the number of leadership and empowerment. In 31 it is 3, the number of light-heartedness and daring. If a woman chooses to wear a bra and a blouse, the norm is to wear the bra under the blouse. If she wears it over the blouse this alters her persona, her social meaning, considerably. For a masculine metaphor, remember the Superman joke: 'If he's so clever, why does he wear his underpants over his tights?' In short, things have an order.

I have deliberately stopped the compound number analysis at 45 because by the time you get to 34 you will have got the idea of how the compounds are analysed and the process will be becoming repetitive. Remember the compound rule – the first number is the premier vibration, the second number is important but less powerful.

Don't forget the positive and negative potential. For example, at its highest potential 45 will embody primarily the order of 4 and secondarily the freedom of 5. At its lowest it will carry the negative elements of 4 (chaos) and 5 (restriction).

The Meaning of the Compound Numbers

10

The 1 and the 0 go to great lengths in the long term, but in the short term they make mistakes, repeat them and often know they are lousing up a brilliant potential. They are often restricted by negative people and are encouraged to continue on their path by making secret plans. It is a wise 10 who comes to realise that it needn't be that way and things not only can but must change.

If it's a car number: The vehicle would benefit from a second opinion from another garage. It may be a simple problem that needs rectifying, not the cause of a series of monster bills.

11

Often regarded as a painful compound or master number, the 11 vibration should nevertheless be welcomed for there is a fine line between excitement and anxiety. The 11 is light in its most positive vibration, and there are few who welcome an excessively bright light in their environment. 11s will often experience jealous people trying to douse their intuitive brightness, either in business or emotionally. Keep the power on, 11, and understand that because someone has a problem with enlightenment you needn't pick up their grief.

If it's a car number: A useful workhorse with much ferrying of others as a natural part of its potential. It may also be sporty and a grudge car, i.e. the envy of jealous admirers.

12

The 12 is an innocent soul who has ability but defers to the opinions of others too easily. The final 3 reduction escalates the need for awareness of duplicity, especially in women, whether the carrier is male or female. To succeed in this vibration the carrier is encouraged to pay extra attention to detail and not to let idleness or slapdash behaviour waste their potential.

If it's a car number: It will need extra maintenance as

performance duties may outweigh its initial purpose. The vehicle is of no use to its owner if he does not regularly maintain it.

13

The connection with the 13's unlucky tag is the combination of the 1 leadership, the 3 lightheartedness and spontaneity and the final reduction: the potential for chaos or order. Phew! With so many distractions the overall vibration could well be akin to the captain being drunk as the ship veers towards the rocks; or, and it is a very important or, the most enjoyable and organised piece of plain sailing. There is much movement and change contained within this compound, and the joy of discovery or the misery of trying to hang on to the finished past is yours.

If it's a house number: This house will need a revolving door, and the Christmas list of its inhabitant will include DIY tools and many home-oriented gifts. The occupants must also be extra diligent with security as the busy lifestyle of this domestic set-up can make them forgetful of small but necessary precautions.

14

A most elemental number in the earth, wind and fire context. Like the weather, the 14 can be warm, sunny, cold and temperamental, all of which is of use somewhere in the world. As Zen says: 'There is never bad weather, only weather.' It just is. With change come new experiences and learning. This is right up the 14 street or country lane. This vibration is about nature, feelings and action.

If it's a house number: A haven for its occupants,

possessing a nurturing vibration which is apparent when it warmly welcomes you in. Romantic smells are in evidence in this home: bread baking, or bubblebath wafting from the bathroom.

15

The 15 vibration is communicative, and if it is a house number the door hinges will be replaced more often than in most homes! The 1 holds individuality and the 5 a vibration of sensuality and beauty. The overall 6 reduction of both numbers gives a leaning towards snobbery and keeping up with the Jones's.

If it's a car number: This vehicle will be an extension of the spare bedroom. Everything will be dumped in it, just in case it's needed, you understand. It's a shoe shop, library and toy shop.

16

This is a number of isolation and of a home-lover. The 16 will not take orders from others easily – preferring to be right is a polite way of putting it. The carrier has a tendency to misuse knowledge, and gossip could assist her in coming a cropper.

If it's a house number: The home of a bookworm. Whereas many people have dust, the occupants of 16 will have books and coffee-table literature. No space for frills, just faded chintz or serviceable comfort.

17

The 17 carries the spiritual and earthly woes on his or her shoulders. Excellent with information and the translating of it, he may work for the good of the community and hold a prestigious position at a later rather than early stage of life. Born to please, he is homely and welcoming.

If it's a house number: It's all windows open, never a door closed and a place of laughter and airiness. Lazy breakfasts in the conservatory feature in this household, along with a preference for designer finishing touches. Expression of wealth is obvious.

18

Here is a number which needs the finer style of life. Extremely organised, you hold the medal for family and recovery. In the last instance you can spend your last penny (and you probably often do) and then find a ten-pound note as you leave the shop. With the final reduction of 9, your love of beauty will make you available to welcoming liaisons which could lead to explosive partings.

If it's a house number: People who inhabit it will tend to treat it like a friend rather than just a shelter. The 18 house may be noted for its neatness and cleanliness no matter what time you call.

19

The individuality of the 1 and bonding influence of the 9 needs acknowledgement and a round of applause in the 19 compound. To understand the final reduction of the restrictions-before-success vibration of the master number 10, the carrier needs to be reminded of her marvellous resources during times of strife.

If it's a house or office number: The indication is one of much renovation, repair or a protracted settling-in period. You will need much energy to fit into the demands of this vibration: it will require work and there may be a delay in acquiring or moving into the property.

20

The caring and wisdom contained within the 20 compound is well placed if the carrier holds a caring or nurturing position. Others may rant and rave, but the 20 will cajole and encourage the errant to get the best out of their higher selves. They work well with others who have lost their will or way. The probation service will benefit from this vibration.

If it's a house number: The associations will be strong and the vibration of the previous owners will linger longer than in most vibrations. This is because of the intensity carried within the 2 vibration and the quality of the zero being an ancient skill carried forward. To find that the house is haunted would not be unexpected, nor should the owner be surprised if previous owners from years gone by have an urge to revisit to reminisce. It will be a home of many happenings and any structural surveys should be thorough.

21

The late developer tag suits the 21 to a T. He may also look much younger than his years, which is odd because the early lifestyle of the 21 may well have been more than a little character-forming. A devilish streak will have taken him into avenues he may cringe at in the fireside years. But there is no substitute for experience and with the 21, with a final reduction of 3, there will be many lessons learned. The carrier often comes up with winning business idea or design.

If it's a house number: It has the symbolic vibration of the bachelor pad with minimalist decor, and gadgetry to save time between dates and appointments. The answer-phone will be the most important feature because the occupants are always out keeping up with the movers and shakers.

22

A most hesitant or destructive number if used in its negative empowerment. Taken to its highest it is diligent, organised and successful in the boardroom. The in-between part of the 22 compound is rare, and you are usually either in it or out of it. You are highly impressionable, and this potential is easily recognised by negative people – do not fall for the old flattery routine. You are encouraged to remember when the Lorelei sings that walking out is much easier than walking back to a relationship.

If it's a house number: The inhabitants will be successful in the marketplace and the home will reflect that success, or their anticipation of it. If the occupants are on the early rungs of success, small *objets d'art* and tasteful purchases will be dotted around the place.

23

Regarded by many numerologists as the most gorgeous number, the 23 has the warmth of the 2 and the love of life of the 3 in its make-up. The final reduction of 23 is 5, and the loving vibration of the 5 adds a sweetness and protection most numbers would envy. The golden path of success is clear for the 23, and any carrier trying to avoid that success could be very frustrated indeed.

If it's a house number: The vibration is to be different and yet everything that one could wish for in a home.

Whether it is a palace or a shack, the vibration is what counts and 23 has cornered the market in the welcome home stakes. Nothing is too much for the owners to do for this house, and the daring it exudes can make it a lovable eyesore in the neighbourhood.

24

Maximise to capitalise: the 2 + 4 compound is not short on the talent for being in the right place at the right time. The 4 at its fullest vibration is careful of detail and the 2 will make the package most appealing in the commercial field and the attraction stakes. Forget the warmth if the negative 24 is at home. They are miserly materialists who will buy food that is well past its sell-by date. What a shame, for their potential is good.

If this is a house number: Everyone will want to visit but few will be invited to. The owners will be quite territorial and skirmishes over 'who was poking around in my . . .?' will be plentiful. A house which was bought for a song and rises in value; a house of the unexpected.

25

Anything to do with the earth – water or land – is the domain of the 25 compound. The highly intuitive final reduction of 7 assists the carrier in market research of any endeavour he or she embarks on. Working on the land with the produce of the land will harmonise this vibration. You are kind and keen on expression of knowledge.

If it's a house number: The vibration will be basic in a farmhouse way: a working/living environment. The inhabitants will know all about struggle, but they will also learn from the experiences along the way.

26

Creativity, kindness and success are well within the realms of the 26 compound, but two less pleasant characteristics have a habit of turning up when a 6 is around and they are snobbery and avarice. There is a rollercoaster feel to this number and the carrier may bite off more than she can chew in financial ventures or property purchases. Steady as she goes, 26.

If it's a house number: The occupants would be well advised to make sure the foundations of their relationship are solid before they embark on living in this vibration – the warmth of this home can make it heart-wrenching to leave.

27

Holders of this compound are entrepreneurial: through their innovations they can bring mankind and technology into line in many ways. Their ability to cut through red tape can be legendary. The carrier must, however, seek the company of like-minded vibrations, perhaps a 9, 18 or 3, and avoid time-wasters.

If it's a house number: A 27 home will be full of interesting and unusual treasures and junk. It has a theatrical already ransacked look, and is as busy as Piccadilly Circus at 5 p.m. on a Friday.

28

Go no further for parenting skills than the potential of the 28 compound. The calmness of the 2 and the spiritual/material curve of the 8 encourage the carrier to steer clear of the stock exchange and its games and allow that rare profession, a great parent, to shine. The final reduction of 2 + 8 is 10, and this shows a

potential for business failure, but then a breakthrough and success eventually, perhaps in a different field.
If it's a house number: The inhabitants may not have much, but what they have they share with anyone who calls. There will always be a cup of tea and a smile here when you have a problem, for they know all about those.

29

The confusion this compound can wreak is substantial, but if you see it through the master number 11 final reduction is worth waiting for. The 2 and 9 conflict can cause dissatisfaction and disappointment if you settle down very early in life. The grass always appears greener for the 29, and common sense needs to be practised. A spiritual path beckons in later life with rewards undreamed of, providing you finish what you've started.
If it's a house number: The vibration is much better for a house or street number because the home features as a welcome stronghold amid the razzmatazz of amorous adventures.

30

Nice number, nice carrier, is generally the rule. The 3 takes risks which others might balk at, but the accompanying 0 will lend stability from a previous incarnation. However, the 30 must be aware of his powerful potential and not use it to gain control over others.
If it's a house number: It will be chosen for its location and contain a plethora of unusual labour-saving devices, leaving the inhabitants more time for caring for mankind and having fun.

31

This number is one of adamant reserve, and one which allows you to be your own counsellor. The 3 + 1 gives an ability to get things done and by yourself. You are not afraid to make your dreams come true and the final reduction of 4 will facilitate that. 31s are not generally good at delegating and can seem aloof. They are very self-contained, and lovers of space.

If it's a house number: Tranquillity plays host in this dwelling and the eclectic artifacts which adorn the premises each have a tale to tell.

32

Good old flirty 32, the number of the hearth and the traveller in many spheres. The 32 compound has the ability to travel the universe in his mind from the fireside chair. Popular and often very attractive, he must not fall for flattery in the commercial and emotional fields. He can be too trusting and overlook glaring evidence of slapdash work and duplicity.

If it's a house number: Working from home is no stranger to number 32, and it may well be the domain of a self-employed individual. The person or persons concerned will have to learn when to draw the line between living and working there.

33

The healer is always present in this very caring compound. 33s are extremely successful in humanitarian causes and when on field work can negotiate and create a better environment for less fortunate others. Tireless workers, they must also be aware that a tired healer is less effective and needs to benefit from sleep like the rest of us. They often collect accolades for their creative good works.

If it's a house number: This home will be a haven for close family and friends of family. It will be the house with the welcoming holly on the door at Christmas, even if the occupants are not Christian!

34

A mixture of dare and do is the vibration of this compound number with a special emphasis on impulsive action. With your head in the clouds and your feet firmly on the ground the respective natures of 3 and 4 indicate fruitfulness in many endeavours as long as the vibrations run alongside each other and not out of control.

If it's a house number: It might be bought for a song and sold for a king's ransom. The kind of house that looks a derelict nightmare, but has such potential. It will not escape excitement but may give the occupants a story or two to tell.

35

Double erratic – and erotic – potential here if the overall potential of colossal success in the final reduction of 8 is ignored. The showbiz quality of this compound can bring great joy or sorrow. The choice is in the hands of the carrier. Think things out and don't bank on spontaneity and freedom as the only things in life.

If it's a house or car number: The repayment or running expenditure can exceed the owner's income.

36

The 36 is highly charged in positive potential if the carrier can take it. This compound shows the beauty of laughter, spiritedness and generosity coupled with creative outlook, ambition and community purpose. The carrier of this number holds an ability to be of service to others and to be rewarded amply.

If it's a house number: A good burglar alarm may be needed to protect the many curios collected within these walls. This vibration suggests the occupant or one of them will travel a lot and the welcome home be warm.

37

Action and thorough knowledge make up this number and the vibration is one of the carriers being quick off the starting block when opportunity is in the vicinity. The final reduction of 10 gives an encouragement which says: 'You will get there no matter what providing you keep good heart.'

If it's a house number: The kind of house where the bedroom is eventually decorated ten years after the occupiers move in. That's the archetypal vibration of 37.

38

The 38 compound has a job to do before reaching the master number 11 final reduction of spiritual enlightenment and knowledge of the inner person, whether it is of yourself or others. The journey of the 38 may be fraught with duplicity and broken promises partnering success, as with the 29. But, like the figurehead on a masted ship, you can also weather the storm and come through, battered and bruised but a winner, during your life path. Stick with it, 38 – the payoff can be stupendous.

If it's a house number: This is a home of understanding and truth after a skirmish or battle with treachery, or being in a contracts race during the purchase of or application for tenancy.

39

You are too trusting by half. The first number 3 in this compound and the 3 final reduction render the carrier vulnerable to bossy or conniving people. Be on your guard as regards the credibility of others and don't carry the can for lazy individuals.

If it's a house number: It's a home that might be neglected by idle occupants. The back garden or surrounding land may be littered with rusting implements and junk.

40

Business success coupled with ancient wisdom gives the 40 compound an advantage over market forces. Providing the carrier sticks to the non-chaotic route, the 40 can bring great rewards, even in matters of family and love. One major point is that the wisdom and understanding 0 brings allows enjoyment of financial acumen, and the 40 will not skimp on lavish sharing.

If it's a house number: It may well be neat, well-painted and cared for. This is a haven for the workaholic.

41

With an ability to collate, lead and love, the 41 is a splendid vehicle in which to discover the planet through travel, exploration or cultural exchanges. The travel writer would be comfortable under this vibration as the need for facts and adventure through the individual's ability to perceive and transfer to paper is strong.

If it's a house number: It will be the core of the

neighbourhood watch or residents' association. A popular number because it contains the orderly 4 and the 1 of
leadership, and the total of the freedom loving 5.

42

A love of the home may tug at the ambitious 4
contained within this compound. Many will envy the
social set-up of the 42, and not for their possessions,
more for their peace of mind. Fashion-conscious at all
levels, the 42 can appear quite selfish on the surface
and may need to be brought down a peg or two by
caring and long-suffering friends. Male carriers will
notice that they adjust their tie a lot or pat their hair;
female carriers will love mirrors.

If it's a house number: Peace and cleanliness are important to this wholesome vibration. There is a tendency to
snobbishness in this household and they may actually *be*
the Joneses.

43

The squabbling potential within the 43 number is high,
and your sense of right and wrong is prominent. You are
cerebral and knowledgeable but in your worst vibration
can be pedantic and dismissive. The psychic ability of the
43 is considerable but so critical can they be that they will
dismiss any precognition as coincidence and lose out on a
learning curve. Because they live so much in the head
they may also lean towards impracticality in electrical
work and plumbing. Leave it to the experts, 43.

If it's a house number: This is the house the neighbours are curious about. Lights on late, people leaving
early in the morning. Occupants may have unusual
professions.

44

The best example to explain the 44 compound would be that of the scientist who finds spiritual enlightenment at some point in his life, usually later. Within this number are two 4s of ambition and the final reduction, 8, is that of balancing the spiritual and the material worlds. The 44 may also encounter great frustration in life and feel cheated if he refuses to look at both sides of opportunity. Greedy when operating negatively, the 44 could be a familiar fixture at the magistrates' court if he chooses the darker side of life.

If it's a house number: This home may have many owner/occupiers due to the state of the finances of the tenants.

45

The 45 contains the positive and negative aspects of the 4's order versus chaos and the 5's freedom versus restriction. This number vibrates well with truth and freedom of information, e.g. scientific matters and inventions for the good of mankind. There is a potential for unfeasible ideas to be followed through because of a build-up of errors.

If it's a house number: The children of this house will have fairies at the bottom of the garden or on the balcony and will convince others kids that they have. There is a secure feeling about this home and its potential is one of balance.

THE MEANING OF EACH LETTER OF THE ALPHABET

A, the first letter of the alphabet and first vowel = 1
When A is the premier (the first and most important) vowel in a first name the carrier is alert, bold and at the hub of life. The gutsy A is the proverbial good man in a storm.

B, the second letter of the alphabet = 2
B is the cuddly, snuggly home-lover. Think of the people with B as the first letter of their names, the Babs', the Bennies, and they are generally friendly types.

C, the third letter of the alphabet = 3
C is the third consonant and its carrier will show vivacity, spontaneity and, if over-confident, sometimes a reckless streak.

D, the fourth letter of the alphabet = 4
D as a premier consonant will display a need for order and tidiness. You will enjoy power but can be a martyr when snowed under.

E, the fifth letter of the alphabet and second vowel = 5
When E is the premier vowel in a first name the carrier is freedom-loving and charming. You might be a chatter-box, and may love the limelight of drama.

F, the sixth letter of the alphabet = 6
F as a premier consonant carries the vibration of the mother hen sharing with her chicks. Creative and stylish.

204

G, the seventh letter of the alphabet = 7
The studious G as a premier consonant will be intuitive,
learned and solitary out of choice.

H, the eighth letter of the alphabet = 8
When H is a premier consonant power and business
success are within the carriers' grasp. They are,
however, also known for deep pockets and short
arms.

I, the ninth letter of the alphabet and third vowel = 9
When I is the premier vowel in a first name the carrier is
sensitive with a mission to bring people and information
together, a catalyst who gets a buzz out of life.

J, the tenth letter of the alphabet = 10/1
J as a premier consonant has the potential to win against
all odds. Your honesty and unyielding desire not to give
up will bring you success – eventually.

K, the eleventh letter of the alphabet = 11/2
K as a premier consonant gives the carrier insights into
the purpose of life which are often missed by others.

L, the twelfth letter of the alphabet = 12/3
L is a doing, feeling and energised vibration which opens
doors to many opportunities. It is no coincidence that
the word 'love' begins with L.

M, the thirteenth letter of the alphabet = 13/4
M as a premier consonant brings the orderly vibration of
the 4. Most carriers will be industrious with a hint of the
workaholic in some cases.

N, the fourteenth letter of the alphabet = 14/5
N introduces a creative and spotlight-loving character.
Great dreamers, they are confident and sometimes
over-optimistic.

**O, the fifteenth letter of the alphabet and fourth vowel =
15/6**
When O is the premier vowel in a first name the carrier
will be community-minded and a good student.

P, the sixteenth letter of the alphabet = 16/7
P as a premier consonant in a name gives the holder a
spiritual teaching ability, which would incorporate philosophical leanings. Plato, Plotinus, Protagoras, Pythagoras: all great thinkers.

Q, the seventeenth letter of the alphabet = 17/8
Q knows all about determination as the 8 vibration
prefers no other outcome than success.

R, the eighteenth letter of the alphabet = 18/9
R as the premier consonant in a name will hold the
potential of the peacemaker and the carrier of facts so
that strife can be soothed.

S, the nineteenth letter of the alphabet = 19/1
S will incorporate new beginnings at many stages of your
life and the added tease of a block before success as the
19 reduces to a 10/1 before analysis.

T, the twentieth letter of the alphabet = 20/2
T as a premier consonant will give the carrier extra
strength to help others and the diplomatic vibration of 2

will make you long-suffering.

U, the twenty-first letter of the alphabet and fifth vowel = 21/3

When U is the premier vowel in a first name you will be freedom-loving, like the carrier of the E vowel, with the bonus of being quick off the mark in business dealings.

V, the twenty-second letter of the alphabet = 22/4

V carries the potential for greatness and the ability to help others on a grand scale. The vibration of the master number 22 and the order-seeking 4 encourages the carrier to be far-seeing and acquisitive. The names Victor and Victoria both mean the victorious winner; Vita means one who loves life.

W, the twenty-third letter of the alphabet = 23/5

W offers a fun-loving, flirtatious, expressive, and hard to pin down vibration.

X, the twenty-fourth letter of the alphabet = 24/6

X as a premier consonant in a name indicates sensuality, a loving nature and the social climbing aspect of the 6 vibration, which can be very snobbish.

Y, the twenty-fifth letter of the alphabet = 25/7

Y affords the carrier the potential of higher mind experiences, but you can miss out through inaction as the shape of the Y indicates: going along and then being unable to decide which road to take when it splits.

Z, the twenty-sixth letter of the alphabet = 26/8
When Z is the premier consonant in a name the carrier is a cornucopia of ability, hope and fruitful associations. Zoe, for example, means giver of life.

WORD VIBRATIONS

Name Vibrations
Names carry so much information about us. The easiest way to visualise the power of the name information is to think of it as the list of ingredients now printed on the packaging of food. The most important ingredient or component comes first, then the rest in descending order of importance.

The following are some examples to show you how quick and easy the process of analysing a name is. The first three letters, be they consonants or vowels, carry the primary influence and so are the most important. When there are two vowels together, as in Gail, Fiona or Briony, a special psyche potential is in effect, the psyche being the centre of power and wisdom within us, our inner truth.

What could be more fitting than to start with Pythagoras?

P Y T H A G O R A S   *Premier vowel A:*
7 7 2 8 1 7 6 9 1 1   I lead, follow me
                        Second vowel O:
                        Strive, coordinate, finish
                        First consonant P:
                        I am spiritual
                        Second consonant Y:
                        I access

I think he lived up to his name, don't you?

A   B   I   G   A   I   L   *Premier vowel A:*
1   2   9   7   1   9   3   I lead, follow me
                        First Consonant B:
                        I feel
                        Second Consonant G:
                        I learn

B   E   N   J   A   M   I   N   *Premier vowel E:*
2   5   5   1   1   4   9   5   Freedom and exploration
                        First consonant B:
                        I feel
                        Second Consonant N:
                        I am confident

E   L   I   Z   A   B   E   T   H   *Premier vowel E:*
5   2   9   8   1   2   5   2   8   Freedom and exploration
                        First consonant L:
                        I can
                        Second consonant Z:
                        I unite

```
F  L  E  U  R        Premier vowel E:
6  3  5  3  9        Freedom and exploration
                     Second vowel U:
                     Immediate action with laughter
                     First consonant F:
                     I delegate
                     Second consonant L:
                     I can
```

Now analyse your own name, and those of some of your friends and acquaintances.

Place Vibrations

Numerology states that everything has a vibration. The swinging sixties terminology 'bad vibes' and 'good vibes' are more than just hippie remarks. Notice how the first example, South Africa's ability number, is 4, the number of order and keeping chaos at bay.

```
S  O  U  T  H     A  F  R  I  C  A
1  6  3  2  8     1  6  9  9  3  1   =   49/4

   N  O  R  T  H     P  O  L  E
   5  6  9  2  8     7  6  3  5   =   51/6
```

The 6 vibration of the North Pole is one of creativity and creation.

```
S  O  U  T  H     P  O  L  E
1  6  3  2  8     7  6  3  5   =   41/5
```

The 5 vibration of the South Pole is in tune with nature and freedom.

Consider the magnetic quality of the two sides and their purpose together as a pair. They make a master number 11, the vibration of light, truth and the energy of two 1s, two equals.

```
A   M   E   R   I   C   A
1   4   5   9   9   3   1       =       32/5
```

The ability number of America, the 'land of the free' is 5, the number of freedom.

```
B   I   R   M   I   N   G   H   A   M
2   9   9   4   9   5   7   8   1   4   =   58/4
```

Birmingham is the industrial capital of the U.K. and lives up well to its industrious 4 ability vibration.

```
S   T       A   L   B   A   N   S
1   2       1   3   2   1   5   1       =       16/7
```

St. Albans carries the vibration of 7, the number of history and knowledge.

As a Roman city St. Albans in Hertfordshire is steeped in ancient history with valuable artifacts and remains of ruins from Roman times when it was called Verulamium. 7 is the number of wisdom, spirituality and learning. The city of St. Albans has always enjoyed a religious reputation and was the home of the first and only British Pope Nicholas Breakspear.

```
L   O   N   D   O   N
3   6   5   4   6   5       =       29/11
```

The bright lights and individuality of the master number 11 vibration may well be why London is such an important major world city. For such a small island, the Prime Minister's office in Downing St. has had such a clout in world affairs for so long. Perhaps things get sorted out in a small town like London . . .

```
M  O  T  H  E  R  W  E  L  L
4  6  2  8  5  9  5  5  3  3   =   50/5
```

As a 5 vibration Motherwell has taken chances and succeeded through the years with workers travelling far and wide to work in her once wealthy mines and steelworks. Any place with 5 Ability number may be down, but not for long. At present Motherwell is wooing light industry.

Motherwell brought prosperity and freedom to many homeless and out of work people as it grew in the industrial revolution. It suits its 5 ability vibration. The Scottish town of Motherwell has played host to at least two major industries over the past hundred years; mining and steel.

```
N  E  W     Y  O  R  K
5  5  5     7  6  9  2   =   39/3
```

Is known as the city that never sleeps and its numerological vibration of 3 suits it as its ability number. Note the freedom seeking three 5s in New, which suggest a dramatic nature.

Key Words in the Human Condition

In life, learning and experience we have several common denominators, things we take for granted such as sun, moon, day, night, weather, faith, trust. The sun rises, the sun sets; the weather, as the Buddhists say, is neither bad nor good, it just is. Oxygen and moisture always turn up. When you analyse the individual and number vibration, be prepared to understand the importance, meaning and purpose of each word. Not only is it of interest to give these words their rightful understanding, it also trains us how to appreciate meaning and number vibration.

$$
\begin{array}{ccccc}
L & I & G & H & T \\
3 & 9 & 7 & 8 & 2
\end{array} \quad = \quad 29/11
$$

Light illuminates, and 11 is the number of illumination and insight.

$$
\begin{array}{cccccccc}
D & A & R & K & N & E & S & S \\
4 & 1 & 9 & 2 & 5 & 5 & 1 & 1
\end{array} \quad = \quad 28/10
$$

Darkness is a negative 10, the vibration of struggle and fearfulness.

$$
\begin{array}{ccc}
G & O & D \\
7 & 6 & 4
\end{array} \quad = \quad 17/8
$$

Represents heaven/spirituality. The figure 8 is balanced: the top part is heaven/spirit, the lower half is the earth/material life.

```
B  U  D  D  H  A
2  3  4  4  8  1   =   22
```

22 is the number of empowerment and 2 the number of using power in a most constructive way.

```
U  N  I  V  E  R  S  E
3  5  9  4  5  9  1  5   =   41/5
```

Universe is a 5 vibration and is the number of freedom of the planet, being in tune with nature.

```
H  E  A  V  E  N
8  5  1  4  5  5   =   28/10
```

```
E  A  R  T  H
5  1  9  2  8   =   25/7
```

If there is any doubt about the meaning of 8, just add heaven and earth: 10 + 7 = 8 – balancing spiritual and material life.

```
Y  I  N
7  9  5   =   21/3
```

```
Y  A  N  G
7  1  5  7   =   20/2
```

When we add yin and yang; 3 + 2 = 5, we get the vibration of energy and freedom.

```
P O S I T I V E
7 6 1 9 2 9 4 5   =   43/7

N E G A T I V E
5 5 7 1 2 9 4 5   =   38/11
```

Together they make a 9 vibration, the number of harmony.

```
        Y O U
        7 6 3   =   16/7

          M E
          4 5   =   9
```

When we add you and me, 7 + 9 = 16 = 7, we get the vibration of analysis. That is exactly what happens when people get together: they make a comparison of how the other's life is lived and they can analyse their own lives in this context.

```
M O T H E R
4 6 2 8 5 9   =   34/7

F A T H E R
6 1 2 8 5 9   =   31/4

  C H I L D
  3 8 9 3 4   =   27/9
```

When we add all three together they make 7 + 4 + 9 = 20/2, the number of home and nurturing.

```
C   H   A   O   S
3   8   1   6   1   =   10
```

Chaos is a 10 vibration, the number of struggle with the potential for success eventually.

PERSONALITY PROFILES

Before you read this next section be encouraged by the obvious fact that each date of birth is ours from the moment we come on to the planet as an individual. Here we are going to look at some individuals we will all recognise, and there is no need to fudge personality profiles simply because the numbers were there before the newspaper headlines.

Placido Domingo: 21/1/1941: 1

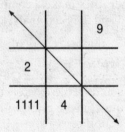

As a life path 1, Placido Domingo will love taking the lead, this is a life path he has followed faithfully by taking the lead in opera so many times. His chart suggests that he is a sensitive man and may choose to be careful of whom he can trust. This is shown in his trait

216

line of cynicism. The four 1s indicate a person who likes to get his point across and he may insist on being heard. A love of material life is his major trait. His mother is prominent in his thoughts or life.

Prince Philip: 10/6/1921: 2

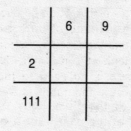

Prince Philip is a typical 2 vibration in that though he is not king he has to do the work of consort to the Queen. The 2 has a support role in life and is no less of a vibration for carrying that number. In this world the roadsweeper is as necessary as the Queen for he gives everyone a more comfortable existence. As a 2 Prince Philip, if operating positively, will be sensitive, cooperative and a soother of woes; if operating negatively he will be tactless and uncaring. His chart suggests a separation from his father and this is something which could affect him deeply throughout his life. The chart also indicates a person who appreciates art and may paint or write well.

Hillary Clinton: 26/10/1947: 3

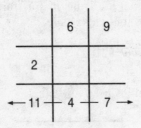

As a life path 3, the First Lady of America will contribute much of the 'you want it done? It's done' vibration of the 3. They are spontaneous and even in analytical mode can fly faster by the seat of their pants than most. She may also be an excellent fundraiser on a grand scale, for the popularity of the 3 opens doors which are considered barred by others. Within a few months of her husband's election as President of the United States people were complaining that she, not he, was running the country. Such is the magnetism of the 3. They are high-profile and sensitive to criticism, but can rise above it with a supportive partner. Quite frankly, wouldn't you prefer the president of the United States' lawyer wife to be working with him rather than against him?

As a 3 Hillary Clinton's verbal skills come into play and as a lawyer she is most definitely in the right profession. She also possesses the potential to be a novelist or biographer. A born communicator, she has been trained via the legal system to be responsible for what she says: long may that be part of her skills. If operating negatively the 3 can come a cropper through acting in haste only to repent at leisure. A negative 3 must avoid scandal. Note that the premier vowel 1 vibration – I join, I care – in both her names matches her husband's.

Martina Navratilova: 18/10/1956: 4

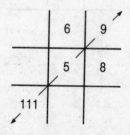

Martina's chart shows that she certainly lives up to her life path as 4 is the number of strategy, form and discipline, three essential ingredients for a world-class tennis player. The 8 within her grid indicates that she will witness and experience many things in life, and as the 8 is in the emotions trait line this certainly has been the case. By looking at her numbers on the grid you will see that she has a strong trait line of determination, a leaning towards independence and her father's/ male role model influence. Note the trait line of universal love indicating by the single 5 her spiritual side. The 6 and 8 in her chart suggest she would make a great television presenter or publisher, and the life

path 4 offers her the potential to be a brilliant businesswoman. Tell me about it! Martina carries the
premier vowel vibration, the psyche vibration, of A:
follow me, I lead.

Mick Jagger: 26/7/1943: 5

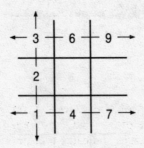

Mick Jagger is the ultimate 5 life path. A man who
needs his freedom with a vengeance in order to create
and constantly restructure his art, his love and his
rebellious non-conformity. 5s need space, drama, sex
'n' drugs 'n' rock 'n' roll. Living in the presence of 5 is
like living in a whirlwind – very, very exciting, if you
can stand the pace! 5s need a match in love, not a
passenger and his liaison with the dynamic Jerry Hall
would be typical.

   As a 5 he will understand its lesson of total destruction, that if you hang on to any addictions for too long
they become overbearing. The experiences and the
outcome of the life path 5 is one of 'Wow, what a trip!'
They do not die wondering . . . Mick has the premier
vowel vibration I: I join, I care.

Prince Edward: 10/3/1964: 6

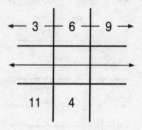

The potential for the Queen's youngest son, Prince Edward, is one of creativity and logic (see the trait line of logic). His chart indicates that he will want to make his own way in the world (see the 6 and 4 in the plane of individuality) and that his mother will be more influential in his life than his father . . .

As a life path 6, Edward will prefer to work with groups of people and, so far, his efforts in the world of theatre have shown just that. Emotionally he has a major lesson to learn (see trait line of over-sensitivity) and that may well be to express himself in a more confident way in matters of the heart. The 3 indicates a caring person but also that he can be a bit sarcastic. The chart also indicates a potential for communication difficulties on the paternal level which will have to be worked out or ignored in order to progress.

Queen Elizabeth II 21/4/1926: 7

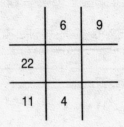

As a life path 7 the Queen has much in common with her daughter-in-law, the Princess of Wales, who is also a 7. Both women have had to break new ground and go it alone in their respective circumstances. As a 7 the Queen knows all about isolation, living above the shop and literally working the same hours as a publican – twenty-four. One does not switch off being Queen at all and the responsibility of being 'owned' by a government as their figurehead must be daunting if not crushing at times. The 7 will know how to be an excellent Defender of the Faith and will allow no one to undermine the task she has been given. 7s are drawn to the serenity of the animal world and shun the material life, would you believe? In fact we have heard many tales of her conserving and economic ways. Her chart further indicates that she is a shy person and is very sensitive to the opinions and remarks of others. The pain of being in the spotlight she does not carry lightly. Her body language verifies this as she reaches out her gloved hands to greet strangers who are nervous too. Knowledge is power to her, and we also have reports of the research she undertakes on who she is to meet, or the history of the place she is to visit. A true 7. Perhaps the elder 7 could assist the younger 7?

Elizabeth carries the premier vowel vibration of E: Freedom, travel and exploration.

Warren Beatty: 30/3/1937: 8

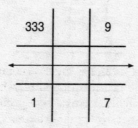

As a life path 8, Warren Beatty is on the planet to follow the path of balance, challenge and material pursuit. A life path more suited to Hollywood would be hard to find. 8s are renowned for their beauty and sensuality, and if you have never heard of Warren Beatty ask your mother . . .

The 8 is no stranger to pain early in life but is able to withdraw and work hard at material compensation until he can learn to trust again. The 8 must learn that money cannot make you happy, but it is a marvellous tool. At some point in their lives spiritual development, nothing heavy, will complete the ultimate existence. The three 3s in Warren's chart indicate a love of women, and by way of understatement he has a major lesson to learn about avoiding being manipulated by women this time round. The 8 gains great satisfaction out of the family and its strengths, and when operating positively has excellent relationships with his offspring.

Fay Weldon: 22/9/1931: 9

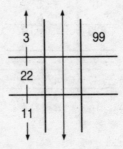

As a life path 9, Fay Weldon is a catalyst, a bringer together of people, information and harmony. When we look at her grid it reveals that her feminine side is very developed and that her mother and women played a more prominent role in her life than her father. In fact, the missing 5 indicates there might be a separation from the father or a loss. Her chart further shows she is logical and has a good sense of humour. However, with that 3 in her chart, she must watch out for jealous females and, even though she is a successful writer, monetary matters will be a learning curve. The two 2s further reveal that she may worry more than is necessary. Her compound number before reduction to 9 is 27. The 2 suggests she is a nurturer and the 7 suggests she is a loner and needs, perhaps enjoys, isolation, although the trait line of dependence shows she enjoys the support of her friends.

Sir Ranulph Twiselton Fiennes: 7/3/1944: 10

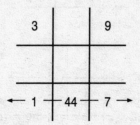

As a master number 10, global explorer Ranulph Fiennes lives up to his life path intention exceedingly well. An ex-soldier, he is an expert in leadership endeavours against all odds and his need to be in charge shows in his choice of profession. The type of life he has chosen again highlights the energy contained within the 10: no matter what the hurdles, I'll get to be number 1. The 3 in his chart indicates a quirky sense of humour and a person who is very caring. The two 4s further indicate that he has to come to terms with money this time round, and of course explorers have to find funding as well as make a living. The 7 in his date of birth indicates a loner and I am sure there is little conversation *en route* to the Poles or riding white water.

Prince Charles: 14/11/1948: 11

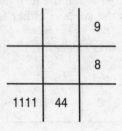

A New Age king if ever there was one, and it might not come as a surprise, considering the caring vibration of the millennium – the year 2000 – if he found himself in that position. His life path is the master number 11, his middle-distance vibration, the month of his birth, another master number 11 and his overview of life, the year of his birth, the master number 22. Prince Charles, then, has the potential to be the stuff of which fairytale kings are made, but with his sensitivity he may also see the 'firm' as an expensive and unrealistic circus. A King, Queen, Prince and Princess would suffice in a stream-lined monarchy, and how many palaces do a queen and king need? He and his wife have an excellent compatibil-ity – she is a 7, he an 11. Together they make a 9 vibration, a relationship with painful separations but always a coming together. Further maturity may well see them together again, for as king and queen they would have no equal. Already the Princess of Wales is a force to be reckoned with in the world and Prince Charles keeps his regal profile low. Theirs has the potential to be a very spiritual (in the true sense) marriage as neither will forego the freedom of their life paths. On another note, in psychology there is a belief that our choice of partner is influenced either positively or negatively by our role model of the opposite sex. The Queen, like the Princess of Wales, is also a 7 life path. Charles holds a premier vowel vibration of A: follow me, I lead.

Robert Maxwell: 10/6/1923: 22

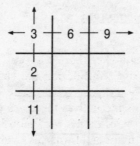

An archetypal master number 22, Robert Maxwell had it all: power, money, family and a life path number which had the potential to teach him how to enjoy and use power to the ultimate good for humanitarian causes. At this point be aware again that when a master number misbehaves or operates negatively it can be the most excruciatingly painful experience, and the rest of Robert Maxwell's story is, as they say, history. When a 22 misuses power, batten down the hatches and pretend you are not in, for 22 is also known as the terrorist number and wreaks havoc when out of control. His day of birth, 10, indicates a struggle at some point in his life

and shows a creative mind which gathers information
well. The 3 in his chart indicates a quick tongue or
sarcasm, with a preference for female company rather
than male. Several years ago I stepped back from a
business proposition from someone with exactly the
same numbers as Robert Maxwell's, though in a different format, and my decision was proven right long
before the Maxwell story unfolded. This does not mean
that everyone with these numbers is hard work, but it
can be a warning.

Dorothy Parker: 22/8/1893: 33

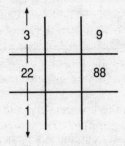

Writer, wit, screenplay writer, bon viveur and social
commentator Dorothy Parker scathed and entertained
her way to the top of the communication ladder, and that
is no surprise, for she was a master number 33, one of
the most eloquent yet painful numbers to carry. Several
marriages and drinks later, she knew all about the
painful aspect of the 33. Reduced to a 6, the 33 is
creative, skilful with her hands and her wordsmithing
abilities. The 33 is marvellous as a healer, and at coping

with problems on a grand scale, but generally not on a home level. Dorothy's generosity as a healer was apparent when upon her death she left her fortune to the Martin Luther King Foundation to advance their human rights cause. The two 3s in her life path number would account for her sarcasm, although many of us have enjoyed her one-liners such as, 'One more drink and I'll be under the host', and of a Katharine Hepburn performance, 'She ran the whole gamut of emotions from A to B.'

MOZART AND NUMEROLOGY

Mozart had a fascination with numerology. Research by Dr Grattan-Guinness of Middlesex University shows the composer's predilection with the numbers 18 and 9 (1 + 8 = 9). It is my personal belief that Mozart was investigating and celebrating the number 9, the vibration of harmony and the ultimate number in ancient numerology.

Mozart lived in the 18th century, and the year he died, 1791, is an 18/9 vibration. *The Magic Flute* unfurls a plethora of examples of 18/9. The High Priest Sarastro in the opera is attended by 18 priests and makes 18 appearances. The contemporary poster advertising *The Magic Flute* was specially designed to have exactly 18 lines – even though some things had to be missed out to achieve this. Mozart's interest and association with freemasonry also interlinks with the frequency of 18 and 9. The word 'mason' itself has a vibration of 9; and freemason = 11: the master number of insight, illumination and matters of the higher mind. One fact is obvious: he was using the Pythagorean system – the Chaldean method does not use the sacred number 9.

It is also interesting that the name Wolfgang Amadeus Mozart is 8, the number of two 0s balanced together. This vibration gives him the ability number of 8, to balance spiritual (the top of 0) and material (the base of 0) efforts in his life.

THE DAY YOU WERE BORN

Cheiro's Way
The Day – the Month – the Year

Cheiro, whose real name was Count Louis Hamon, used the ancient Chaldean method, which differs in alphabetic layout and meaning from the Pythagorean way of numerology. Cheiro drew attention to the importance of the day of birth, and I agree heartily with him on that extremely vital aspect of numerology, but prefer to analyse it through the Pythagorean method. The day of our birth is the first fact known about us: as we emerged into the world – and long before scanners were invented – we were more than halfway out before the obstetrician or midwife knew what sex we were. The fact that we were being born on that special day is etched in the universe's birthday book.

Below are listed the numbers of the days of the month and their potential, from the best to the worst vibration.

1st: Fortuitous, strident, productive, spiteful, nit-picking, destructive
2nd: Homely, genial, rhythmic, sedentary, timid, sly, devious
3rd: Spontaneous, daring, loving, confused, critical, neurotic

4th: Diligent, loyal, disciplined, over-worked, slapdash, mulish, dictatorial

5th: Freedom-loving, wide-ranging, esoteric, frustrated, uncertain, libidinous, dangerous

6th: Home-maker, family values, kind, humanitarian, opinionated, officiating, bombastic

7th: Intuitive, thinker, religious, eccentric, isolated, uncoordinated, over-assertive, braggart

8th: Hard-working, honest, strong, insecure, bossy, tyrannical

9th: Caring, harmonious, adventurous, turgid, time-waster, over-demanding, alcoholic

10th: Individualistic, vital, secure, motivated, impotent, indifferent, low self-esteem

11th: Psychic, illuminating, healer, tactless, hypocritical, fanatical, obsessive

12th: Inspired, comical, considerate, manipulating, conceited, big-headed

13th: Dutiful, positive, encouraging, frazzled, unsure, uncouth

14th: Multi-faceted, entrepreneurial, daring, vivacious, shallow, unpredictable, psychotic

15th: Cosseting, sincere, peaceful, petty, disorganised, sulky, martyrish

16th: Philosophical, educated, informed, faithless, ungainly, obstructive, longing

17th: Honouring, candid, respectable, careless, disinterested, stubborn, touchy

18th: Kind, truthful, accommodating, compassionless, unfaithful, fixed, sly, egotistical, two-timing

19th: Dependable, winner, innovative, idle, submissive, greedy

20th: Helpful, easy-going, without side, inactive, easily bullied, people-pleasing, gossip

21st: Gregarious, lively, expressive, random, gossipy, troublemaker, ill-tempered, liar

22nd: Forthright, far-sighted, organised, resolute, deceitful, cruel, dangerous

23rd: Country-loving, conservationist, flexible, musical, dreary, riveted, dull, hyperactive, ill-informed

24th: Vigorous, genial, doer, ethical, snobbish, traitor, resentful, used

25th: Investigative, informed, spiritual, teacher, accident-prone, bigoted

26th: Efficient, forceful, reliable, balanced, slothful, under-developed, frigid

27th: Generous, fair, catalytic, self-sacrificing, social, quaint, embarrassing, jealous, greedy, divides and rules

28th: Dynamic, motivated, leader, drained, fanciful, pompous, Walter Mittyish

29th: Charmed, versatile, open, masked, secretive, petty, unreliable

30th: Keen, optimistic, bountiful, expansive, tedious, indiscreet, depressed

31st: Consistent, orderly, neat, relentless, negligent, inflexible, narrow, secretive

Why do we celebrate birthdays and why do card manufacturers create cards in such millions? Just a bunch of numbers? I think not. The birthday is a celebration and an annual acknowledgement of the lessons we have agreed to come into life to study. Isn't it hurtful when a close family member forgets to send us a 50p birthday card? And the rows when a spouse forgets to surprise us on the anniversary of the day we were born! Something inside us remembers the importance of being born and doesn't want to be forgotten.

Like the high-powered executive job, the birthday allows us a yearly assessment of our progress so far. The boozy, food- and gift-oriented birthdays are fine, but underneath it is a spiritual day and at some point I strongly advise setting some time aside to get in touch with the part of you that understands why you are here and what your purpose is. Everything you are is inside your DNA, the centre of power and wisdom which knows what to do and how to do it. Talk with and to it. We are less complex than advertising or new medicine (my word for science) would have us believe. Have faith in you, for you are a universe, a library of information. The numbers you carry are your library cards.

The Inspirational Power of Colour

Colours which enhance and inspire your life path number

Numerologists believe that your day of birth number corresponds to a colour number – for example, if you were born on 12 March your colour number would be 1 + 2 = 3. We all have our favourite colours, but have you ever thought why? Maybe it's because they enhance our auras, or simply how we feel about ourselves. In recent years more has been done to nurture our natural responses to colour in the environment than at any time in our evolution: colour in healing, colour in astrology, colour in the home to make it a more harmonious place in which to live. The importance of this natural response within us is not lost on paint manufacturers, who go to great lengths to stimulate our choice and in-built recognition of shades through exotic names such as Guards

Red, California Sage, Mediterranean Blue, Winsome Wheat and so on.

Take your bedroom as an example of the psychology of colour. If you dislike the colour, what a disadvantage it is: it's the last thing you see before falling asleep and the first sight to greet you when you wake in the morning.

The colours which enhance our lives are:

1. Winter white, creamy orange, bejewelled reds, vermilion
2. Dark blues, silver, grey, warm pinks, pearl white
3. Charcoal, lavender, lilac, maroon, violet
4. Emerald green, cobalt blue, turquoise, indigo
5. Heliotrope, burgundy, tangerine, vivid reds, orange, maroon
6. Forest green, Havana brown, midnight blue, French blue
7. Metallic blues, pastel blue, aquamarine, silver
8. All shades of the night – midnight blue, black, indigo – highlighted by opal and silver
9. Tomato red, scarlet, dark orange, gold
10. Watermelon, magenta, off white, silver and gold mixed
11. Coral, cream, pale grey, navy, salmon pink, flashes of lavender
22. Mediterranean blue, indigo, lavender in small quantities, Lincoln green
33. Chartreuse, cocoa brown, French navy, purple

The Day on Which You Were Born

The day of the week on which you were born is important too. According to the original wording of the Florence Ward rhyme:

> Monday's bairn is fair of face,
> Tuesday's bairn is full of grace.
> Wednesday's bairn is full of woe,
> Thursday's bairn has far to go.
> Friday's bairn is loving and giving,
> Saturday's bairn works hard for a living,
> But the bairn born on a Sunday is bonny,
>   blithe and gay.

We gather information about human beings in many ways, and this poem is but one of them. In West Africa, where the rhyme is probably not known, babies are given a name which identifies the day on which they were born. I have used the ability number, the vowel and consonant vibrations, reduced to a single digit for analysis. Let's look at the numerical value of each day to see if you can identify with the vibration of the day of your birth. If you don't know on which day you were born take a look in an astrological ephemeris, which can be found in a library or purchased at any good bookshop or astrological outlet. Also included are the planetary influences for the purposes of comparison.

The Numerical Vibration of Each Day

M	O	N	D	A	Y		
4	6	5	4	1	7	=	27/9

Monday is the moon's day and the moon governs water, fruit, emotions, cycles, fertility and passion. 9 is the number of balance, sensuality, keeping perspective, responsibility, giving selflessly and welcome.

```
      T U E S D A Y
      2 3 5 1 4 1 7   =   23/5
```

Tuesday is Tiew, the god of war's day. It is ruled by Mars, which governs battles, tension, tempers, flare-ups and fire. 5 is the number of freedom, extracting oneself from restriction, expression and action with purpose.

```
    W E D N E S D A Y
    5 5 4 5 5 1 4 1 7   =   37/10
```

Wednesday is Woden's day, the chief god in German mythology. It is ruled by Mercury, the planet of information, facts, calculations, communications and education. 10 is the number of persevering until things equate, persistence, taking the bull by the horns and spiritedness.

```
      T H U R S D A Y
      2 8 3 9 1 4 1 7   =   35/8
```

Thursday is Thor's – Thunder's – day, ruled by Jupiter, the planet of law enforcement, scientific breakthrough, missions, ritual and banking. 8 is the number of capability, loyalty, strength and resourcefulness.

```
F R I D A Y
6 9 9 4 1 7   =    36/9
```

Friday is the day of Freia, the wife of Tiew. It is ruled by love and Venus, the planet of amour, harmony, beauty, grace, charm, sexuality, aromas and delightful exchanges. 9 is the number of harmony, humanitarianism, benevolence, coordinating, the love of art and appreciation of creativity.

```
S A T U R D A Y
1 1 2 3 9 4 1 7   =    28/10
```

Saturday is the day of Saturn, the planet of hardship, prevarication, misunderstanding and worry, and is generally the most violent day of the week according to police statistics. 10 is the number of getting through after a struggle or setback. When vibrating negatively it is about slothfulness, fear and paralysis.

```
S U N D A Y
1 3 5 4 1 7   =    21/3
```

Sunday is the Sabbath, the day of the sun. The sun rules power, light, achievement, ability, energy and warmth. 3 is the number of the Trinity, Father, Son and Holy Ghost; caring, cordiality and responsiveness.

AND FINALLY . . .

Through numerology you have a tool to assist you in your quest for the meaning of life. The menu of numbers I talked of at the beginning of the book will be better understood now, and its importance apparent. No one can tell your story better than you; no one can be you better than you, though many will try to override your right.

The truth is that we have a right to proceed on our life paths, follow our lessons to be learned, no matter how wrong others get it. The 'others' can include lousy parents, critical teachers and partners chosen in haste, blackmail or error. If you recognise any of these, don't think you can't rectify it now – it is never too late to activate your potential as a worthwhile human being. Imagine being on your deathbed and realising that you were responsible for ruining yours or another's life. Not an epitaph many would brag about.

The energy and the courage to make beneficial change is always available, no matter what the circumstances, and much unhappiness is a choice, not an affliction.

There are no such things as unlucky numbers, just a positive or negative vibration route to choose from each one. I hope you have enjoyed this book in the spirit of love for the human race and universe in which it was written. Congratulate yourself for getting this far in your curiosity about you.

Glossary of Terms

Ability number: Shows the capabilities of and suggested occupations for the carrier's name vibration. It is reached by adding the numerical values of both the consonants and the vowels within the name, whether it is that of a person, a company, a house, a city or a car. JOHN SMITH = $1 + 6 + 8 + 5 + 1 + 4 + 9 + 2 + 8 = 44; 4 + 4 = 8$.

Compatability number: How one's life path number relates to another's (life path 5 + life path $7 = 5 + 7$ compatible). It assesses the potential for a good, comfortable personal or working relationship.

Compound numbers: The compound analysis in numerology is the unreduced potential of two digit numbers after 9, from 10 to 99. These are also used to provide extra information when a birthday falls on or between the 10th and 31st of the month. Compound numbers are also useful in analysing business or home addresses.

Grid: The nine-square framework into which we insert our numbers to make analysis easier. There are three vertical and three horizontal columns in the grid.

Insight numbers: When we add our life path and our ability number we reach the insight number, which is of

239

value for analysis after the age of 36. It gives us an opportunity to look at the whole picture so far instead of plodding on and magnifying our errors. For life path 5 and ability number 10 the insight number is 6: $5 + 10 = 15$; $1 + 5 = 6$.

Karmic debts: see Missing numbers.

Life path number: The purpose in this lifetime. Found by adding together the digits of the full date of birth and reducing by further addition to reach a single digit except when the reduction results in the master numbers 10, 11, 22 and 33. For example, $15/7/1972 = 1 + 5 + 7 + 1 + 9 + 7 + 2 = 32$; $3 + 2 = 5$.

Master numbers: 10, 11, 22 and 33 – numbers which carry an extra lesson to learn or message to impart. A master number is not usually reduced unless the carrier is finding it difficult to accommodate.

Missing numbers: Numbers from 1 to 9 which are not included in a name vibration. They are also known as karmic debts, weaknesses which have been brought over into this lifetime to be acknowledged and strengthened. They are found by placing all the vowel and consonant vibrations in a grid and noting which ones are missing.

J	O	H	N		S	M	I	T	H
1	6	8	5		1	4	9	2	8

	6	9
2	5	88
11	4	

John Smith's missing numbers are 3 and 7, two weaknesses to work on.

Multiple numbers: In a date of birth recurring numbers accentuate a trait in the carrier. Two instances of the same number suggests a comfortableness with the vibration of that number in its relative box; multiples over two indicate a pressure to be acknowledged and dealt with in this vibration.

Persona number: In psychology the persona is the exterior expression, the self the carrier wishes the world to see, sometimes in preference to their true inner feelings or intentions. The persona number is reached by adding together the numerical value of the consonants in the name and reducing to a single digit. JOHN SMITH = $1 + 8 + 5 + 1 + 4 + 2 + 8 = 29; 2 + 9 =$ master number 11.

Personal day: An analysis of a twenty-four-hour period. To find the potential of any given day, add the day date to the month in question and the current personal year and reduce. 8 September personal year 6: $8 + 9 + 6 = 23$; $2 + 3 = 5$. A personal hour can also be calculated: day + month + hour in question + personal year.

Personal month: Indicates the potential vibrations in any given month. It is found by adding the digit(s) of the month in question to your current personal year and reducing. So, if you want to find out the potential of March and your current personal year is 9: $3 + 9 = 12$; $1 + 2 = 3$.

Personal year: The year vibration; the year for certain potentials to be realised. It is found by adding the digits of the day, month and year of last birthday. This is an excellent way of analysing how you handled things in the past as well as planning for the future. $1 + 5 + 7 + 1 + 9 + 9 + 9 + 8 = 40$; $4 + 0 = 4$.

Pinnacle numbers: The numbers which show us the four marker years; special years when we get a chance to take stock or in which major events or changes take place. They are based on the twenty-seven years of maturity and analysed in the nine-year numerology life cycle thereafter. Most people mature at a different age and in psychology Freud postulates that we gain insight around the age of thirty-five. The closest to this in the numerological life cycle is $4 \times 9 = 36$. To reach the first pinnacle year subtract the life path number from 36. For life path 5, $36 - 5 = 31$. For the other three, add nine (another life cycle): $31 + 9 = 40$; $40 + 9 = 49$; $49 + 9 = 58$.

Psyche number: Gives us a rare insight into our true selves, our secret selves. This number is without mask and works hand in glove with the life path. It is reached by adding together the numerical values of the vowels. JOHN SMITH = 6 + 9 = 15; 1 + 5 = 6.

Reincarnation: When a soul transmigrates and takes up 'house' in a new body and lifetime.

Reservoir number: A major lesson you learned well in a past life, a credit you start with this time round. It is found by subtracting your life path number from 9 and reducing as necessary. Master number carriers should reverse the process and subtract 9 from their life path number; 9 life path carriers have no reservoir numbers.

Synchronicity: Something which is stronger than chance. A simultaneous action or event.

Trait lines: Horizontal, vertical and diagonal lines which cross the grid and reveal various character traits.

Vibration: A distinctive influence or characteristic surrounding a certain number or period of time in a day, month or year number.

Sexual Awareness

Enhancing Sexual Pleasure

Barry and Emily McCarthy

ILLUSTRATED   NEW UNEXPURGATED EDITION

This book is written to show individuals and couples how to enhance their sexual pleasure. It is focused on feelings and fulfilment, and emphasizes a joyful expression of sexuality and intimacy.

The path to a new awareness includes chapters on:
The Pleasure of Touching
Self-Exploration
Increasing Arousal For Women
Becoming Orgasmic
Learning Control
Overcoming Inhibition

With the current emphasis on the importance of just one sexual partner, this is a timely publication designed to show you just how to make the most of that relationship, and how to build a new sexual partnership.

NON-FICTION/REFERENCE   0 7472 3561 9

More Non-Fiction from Headline:

PECKISH BUT POOR

CAS CLARKE

Delicious Budget Recipes by the Author of *Grub on a Grant*

Cas Clarke's *Grub on a Grant* was hugely popular with students struggling with a single saucepan and a grant. *Peckish but Poor* is for would-be cooks who are ready to move on to more adventurous cookery and want to produce tasty meals on a still restricted budget.

The emphasis here is on easy-to-follow recipes using fresh produce with chapters giving recipes for spring, summer, autumn and winter showing how simple it is to make cheap and delicious dishes by keeping to food that is in season.

If you're short of time, money or experience, you'll find the uncomplicated, no-nonsense recipes in *Peckish but Poor* a brilliant way to build your confidence in the kitchen.

GRUB ON A GRANT
'...a useful little book for the absolute beginner.'
Prue Leith, *Guardian*
'...she reckons her recipes are foolproof, and so they are.' *Daily Telegraph*

NON-FICTION/COOKERY   0 7472 3937 1

A selection of non-fiction from Headline

THE *INDEPENDENT* BOOK OF ANNIVERSARIES	George Beal	£8.99 ☐
MEAN BEANS	Cas Clarke	£5.99 ☐
ENCYCLOPEDIA OF FORENSIC SCIENCE	Brian Lane	£7.99 ☐
JUST THE ONE: The Wives and Times of Jeffrey Bernard	Graham Lord	£6.99 ☐
MALE SEXUAL AWARENESS	Barry McCarthy	£5.99 ☐
BURNS: A Biography of Robert Burns	James Mackay	£8.99 ☐
WORLD ENCYCLOPEDIA OF 20TH CENTURY MURDER	Jay Robert Nash	£8.99 ☐
PLAYFAIR FOOTBALL ANNUAL 1993-94	Jack Rollin (Ed)	£3.99 ☐
HEART AND SOLE	David Sole with Derek Douglas	£5.99 ☐

All Headline books are available at your local bookshop or newsagent, or can be ordered direct from the publisher. Just tick the titles you want and fill in the form below. Prices and availability subject to change without notice.

Headline Book Publishing PLC, Cash Sales Department, Bookpoint, 39 Milton Park, Abingdon, OXON, OX14 4TD, UK. If you have a credit card you may order by telephone – 0235 831700.

Please enclose a cheque or postal order made payable to Bookpoint Ltd to the value of the cover price and allow the following for postage and packing:
UK & BFPO: £1.00 for the first book, 50p for the second book and 30p for each additional book ordered up to a maximum charge of £3.00.
OVERSEAS & EIRE: £2.00 for the first book, £1.00 for the second book and 50p for each additional book.

Name ....

Address ....

....

....

If you would prefer to pay by credit card, please complete:
Please debit my Visa/Access/Diner's Card/American Express (delete as applicable) card no:

Signature .... Expiry Date ....